EXPLORATIONS IN THE
EVOLUTION OF CONGRESS

EXPLORATIONS IN THE EVOLUTION OF CONGRESS

by H. Douglas Price

edited by Nelson W. Polsby

Institute of Governmental Studies Press
University of California, Berkeley
1998

Library of Congress Cataloging-In-Publication Data

Price, Hugh Douglas.
    Explorations in the evolution of Congress / by H. Douglas Price ;
edited by Nelson W. Polsby.
        p. cm.
    Includes bibliographical references.
    ISBN 0-87772-384-2
    1. United States. Congress. I. Polsby, Nelson W. II. Title.
JK1021.P75 1998
328.73--dc21
                                                 98-41407
                                                 CIP

ACKNOWLEDGMENTS

The editor and publisher would like to thank Judith Emerson Price, Professor John R. Price, and Professor Kenneth Shepsle for making material available and for encouraging this project.

CONTENTS

Foreword
    Nelson W. Polsby   ix

Introduction
    Richard F. Fenno, Jr.   xiii

I.   Elections and the Development of Congressional Careers

Chapter 1:	The Electoral Arena	3
Chapter 2:	The Congressional Career Then and Now	33
Chapter 3:	Congress and the Evolution of Legislative Professionalism	53
Chapter 4:	House Turnover and the Counterrevolution to Rotation in Office	75
Chapter 5:	Organizing by Party, Committees by Seniority, and Voting by Coalition	103

II.   In the Literature: Two Critical Looks

Chapter 6:	History of Ethics in Congress: Three Perspectives	129
Chapter 7:	New Perspectives on Wilson's Congressional Government	143

III.   Methods of Inquiry

Chapter 8:	Are Southern Democrats Different? An Application of Scale Analysis to Senate Voting Patterns	161

IV.   Research and Publications of H. Douglas Price   197

Index   203

FOREWORD

The social sciences have rarely been considered fit objects for study as intellectual history.[1] This, I think, will be a temporary phenomenon, in light of the prodigious growth of this luxuriant branch of learning since World War II, its exfoliation into specialties and subspecialties, its expression in university departments, and research institutes, and schools of thought, its intellectual trends and hot spots, texts and syntheses, blind alleys and fruitful innovations. Sooner or later, perhaps a generation from now, scholars will want to look at the growth and diversification of modern social scientific knowledge as a cultural artifact—or as many cultural artifacts. For the moment, we are possibly too close to the origins to be able to sort things out properly. But we can prepare the ground.

In the subspecialty of political science known as congressional studies, there was a sharp upturn after World War II in the number and quality of books and articles in which the political behavior of Congress became the focus of attention rather than its legal or constitutional powers or its administrative machinery or its alleged inadequacies as a vessel of responsible party government.[2] The largest group of scholars displaying the new focus was political scientists who had been associated with the Congressional Fellowship Program of the American Political Science Association or were students of Ralph K. Huitt at the University of Wisconsin.

Although Huitt never wrote a book,[3] his grasp of the nuances and the realities of congressional politics was exceptional, and his teaching was frequently spellbinding. Three other contemporaries of his, David Truman,

---

[1] Honorable exceptions might include: H. Stuart Hughes, *Consciousness and Society* (New York: Octagon, 1976); Stanley Edgar Hyman, *The Tangled Bank* (New York: Atheneum, 1962).

[2] See, e.g., George B. Galloway, *Congress at the Crossroads* (New York: Crowell, 1946) or such titles as *Congress on Trial* (New York: Harper, 1949) by James MacGregor Burns.

[3] His work on Congress was collected posthumously and makes a very interesting book. See Ralph K. Huitt, *Working Within the System* (Berkeley: IGS Press, 1990). An earlier, less complete assembly of his work can be found in Huitt and Robert L. Peabody, *Congress: Two Decades of Analysis* (New York: Harper and Row, 1969).

Stephen K. Bailey, and Lewis Anthony Dexter, wrote important works incorporating the study of Congress into the discipline-wide movement focusing on political behavior, but none of the three ever produced many students. *The Congressional Party: A Case Study*[4] was Truman's last major scholarly effort before he became a senior member of the administration at Columbia, and later president of Mount Holyoke College. This deprived the world of scholarly endeavor in American politics of one of the sharpest minds of his time and one of its most generous teachers. Bailey, deservedly, won a major prize for his evocative *Congress Makes a Law*,[5] a careful case study requiring 400 interviews. At the time of publication, Bailey was on the faculty of Wesleyan University, which had no graduate students in political science. While at Wesleyan, Bailey took a great interest in practical politics, and he served as mayor of Middletown, Connecticut, before moving on to Princeton, and not long thereafter, to Syracuse where he became dean of the Maxwell School of Citizenship. Dexter was an immensely prolific maverick, whose doctorate in sociology was long delayed at Columbia because of a conflict with his supervisory committee.[6] He never stayed long enough at one teaching job to accumulate a body of students, but his writings about Congress, many of them employing a quasi-anthropological style of observation and exhaustive interviewing, were held in very high esteem by the next cohort of scholars, who passed his unpublished manuscript (which later was accepted as his doctoral dissertation), "Congressmen and the People They Listen To,"[7] around among themselves Samizdat-style or tracked his early articles in out-of-the-way journals.[8]

---

[4]New York: Wiley, 1959.

[5]New York: Columbia University Press, 1950.

[6]Dexter (born 1915) was granted the Ph.D. in 1960.

[7]This dittoed manuscript was dated 1956. A condensed version was later incorporated into Raymond Bauer, Ithiel deSola Pool, and Lewis A. Dexter, *American Business and Public Policy* (New York: Atherton, 1963). See also Dexter, *The Sociology and Politics of Congress* (Chicago: Rand McNally, 1969).

[8]For instance, "The Representative and His District," and "When the Elephant Fears to Dance Among the Chickens: Business in Politics? The Case of du Pont," first appeared in *Human Organization*, respectively, vol. 16 (Spring, 1957): 2-13, and vol. 19, no. 4 (Winter, 1960-61): 188-94. This is the journal of the Society for Applied Anthropology.

The next generation saw a very substantial increase in scholarly activity on Congress. The intellectual examples of Huitt, Truman, Bailey, and Dexter were available and greatly admired, and emulated by such eminences as Richard F. Fenno, Jr., Charles O. Jones (the two congressional scholars of their generation to become presidents of the American Political Science Association) and many others. The Congressional Fellowship Program also exposed a small group of political scientists each year to the detailed workings of Congress. Among the earliest and most imaginative of these scholars was Hugh Douglas Price. By the time he entered the program in 1957-58, Price had already completed a brilliant short book, *The Negro in Southern Politics*.[9] This was originally his master's essay supervised by William Carleton and Manning Dauer at the University of Florida. Price's Ph.D. dissertation, which he did at Harvard with V. O. Key, Jr., was both substantively interesting and methodologically innovative for the political science of the 1950s. Its purpose was to demonstrate the utility of scales for political analysis, but it can be read today also as a beautiful illustration of a phenomenon of great importance in congressional life in the 1950s, showing how in roll calls Dixiecrats differentiated themselves from mainstream Democrats.

In a teaching career—at Columbia, Syracuse, and, for 30 years, at Harvard—that extended from the 1950s until his tragic death in a freak household accident in December 1996, Price published very little. Indeed, his master's thesis was to be his only book. Nobody would have predicted this outcome who knew Price in the late 1950s and could observe the breadth of his empirical knowledge, his pedagogical inventiveness, and in particular his capacity to crunch the myriad historical details effortlessly at his command into plausible reconstructions of trends in institutional behavior. These wonderful gifts, though never brought to fruition in the conventional book length format, nevertheless exercised a significant intellectual influence both on his students[10] and on his contemporaries in congressional studies. The purpose of this book is to preserve the record of this influence by gathering up the bulk of his shorter writings so that future

---

[9](New York: New York University Press, 1959).

[10]See, for example, John F. Manley, *The Politics of Finance* (Boston: Little Brown, 1970); and Elaine Swift, *The Making of an American Senate* (Ann Arbor: University of Michigan Press, 1996).

readers can admire the sparkle of one of our most creative minds and appreciate his contributions to our common fund of knowledge.

This collection does not include all his work on Congress, as a glance at the bibliography will confirm. He also wrote with insight about political parties and local political development. Doug was notoriously diffident about publication, and some of his work exists in several unpublished versions. When there is a substantial overlap in subject matter between articles, we have chosen the more complete version. Additionally, one or two holders of copyright to Doug's work wanted more money to reprint than our budget could afford. Despite these limitations, we are happy to have been able to put together this book. In a few places, we could not locate a proper citation for a work mentioned in the text, but otherwise when necessary we have supplied annotation, as Doug surely would have done before publishing.

Doug was exceptionally kind to students. He was an uncommonly thoughtful colleague as well, making it a practice to send flurries of aptly chosen newspaper and magazine clippings to friends on topics that he knew interested them. As someone who knew him for nearly 40 years, and held him in great affection, I can say also that he was afflicted by bad moods, which no doubt affected not only his productivity but also, on occasion, his academic judgment. Early in his career he was deeply unhappy teaching at Columbia, and he escaped gratefully to Syracuse. It came as a surprise to many of us that his later years at Harvard were again clouded by professional dissatisfactions. He had by then contributed such interesting insights to the intellectual framework of the emerging study of Congress, especially to our understanding of the history of the institution, and to sustaining his generation of congressional scholars and the next, that it was hard to reconcile our view of his professional standing with his pessimism. This book, Doug's last flurry of clippings, is meant as a gift to future students of Congress wherein they can glimpse for themselves the strategic value of his contribution.

—*Nelson W. Polsby*

INTRODUCTION

A personal reminiscence, on the occasion of a memorial roundtable in honor of Doug Price at the annual convention of the American Political Science Association, August 1997.

I grew up in political science with Doug Price. We never shared any institutional affiliations; but we shared an interest in American politics. He was a lifetime friend and a lifetime mentor. We met in the early 1960s, as members of a small group of young political scientists who came together to share the excitement of our budding research on Congress. We got a grant to get together periodically in Washington to take members of Congress to dinner and talk about how to study Congress. There were eight of us—Doug, Chuck Jones, Nelson Polsby, Bob Peabody, Milt Cummings, Randall Ripley, Joe Cooper and myself—"the Boys of Congress." I can't recall how we got that grant, but since V. O. Key was chair of the granting committee, and Doug and Milt were students of his, I'm sure Doug had something to do with it.

Anyway, Doug stood out in our little group. He was our most knowledgeable political historian and our most accomplished statistician. He had already pioneered the use of advanced statistical methods in his Ph.D. study of roll call voting in the Senate, using scaling techniques. From his work with Key, he had already developed an interest in the partisan realignments of the 1890s; and that research had led him to the study of changing congressional careers.

His subsequent work on both these subjects was path-breaking; and I can recall a couple of my seminar students, Dave Rohde and Mo Fiorina, cutting their teeth on his career studies—and getting their first published article from an elaboration of his work. At the time of his death, he was developing a different perspective on critical elections, one that focused less on partisan realignment and more on the institutional and policy consequences of such realignments—which, he felt, would refocus our historical research from the 1890s to the Wilsonian period. In my judgment, he was the premier political science historian of American politics of our generation.

I think it was Doug's combination of historical reach and analytical talent that enabled him—more than the rest of us "boys"—to get himself inside whatever problem each of us was wrestling with and to make constructive comments about it. Which he did. In later years, I often expressed the view that if I could choose my Ph.D. thesis advisor from among all the political scientists I ever knew, I'd surely choose Doug Price. And more than just his intellectual capabilities would be involved in that choice. For he was as genuinely kind and generous and selflessly helpful as a colleague could be. The scholarly manifestation of these admirably human qualities—as we all know—was the stream of notes, tear sheets, citations, flotsam and jetsam—even whole books! that he mailed to each of us in accordance with our research interests. He was a wide ranging, voluminous, cross-disciplinary reader, and it was as if he carried each one of us and our research focus in his head while he read—an amazing kind of collegial, other-regardingness rare in any business. Everyone on the receiving end of his memos was, in effect, his graduate student. So while I never had him as a thesis advisor, I did have him as advisor for a lifetime.

A couple of examples: When I was finishing my 1960s manuscript on the politics of the appropriations process, Doug came over to Rochester from Syracuse and spent a long day—into the night—at the house critiquing the manuscript and talking about it. It was an incredibly helpful and stimulating day. And it was his idea—not mine. In the 1990s, when I sent him a copy of my book on Dan Quayle and, again, the one on Mark Andrews, he responded with scattergrams showing me how I could have clarified my distinction between the partisan and personal components of their support. In both cases, he had spent a day in the library, he said, collecting the necessary data. Accompanying the Andrews scattergram was an elaborate causal analysis, recreating the book's entire argument with boxes and arrows—a typical Price effort to help you think about a complex set of relationships. He had an uncanny ability to see where your argument was going and where it could be improved.

Earlier this year, I began to visit a congressional district in Indiana, centered around the city of Muncie. Doug Price knew more about Muncie, Indiana, than any scholar in the country (outside of Ball State University) since he had revisited Muncie as a critic of Lynd's monumental study of Middletown. I was looking forward to talking with him about my new research there and getting his guidance. I'll never get the chance. And that realization only underlines the terrible suddenness of his passing and my larger sense of irreplaceable personal loss.

In helping others, Doug was a marvelous critic. In doing his own work, he was a perfectionist and reluctant to let it go—just because, I have sometimes thought, he was such an effective critic. The fact of the matter, however, is that because he gave so much of himself to others, there is such an obvious abundance of Doug Price's wisdom among us here in this room. And that is a very warm memory for us to live with.

—*Richard F. Fenno, Jr.*

I. Elections and the Development of Congressional Careers

Chapter 1

The Electoral Arena

The conditions of entry into a legislative body and of survival through successive terms are a major factor in the behavior of aspirants and incumbents. In turn, the career perspectives and ambitions of House and Senate members go a long way toward giving structure to those bodies. Looked at the other way, proposals for changes in the structure or procedure of Congress are likely to have a direct impact on the careers of individual members. Some types of changes in the institution are likely only when changes are made in the risks and rewards of the legislative career, either in Congress or in the constituencies. An understanding of the risks of the electoral arena is vital for an understanding of Congress.

Two basic and divergent trends have shaped the pattern of congressional careers in the twentieth century. The first has been the *democratization of the Senate,* brought about by the adoption of direct election of senators, the spread of the direct primary, and the growth of effective two-party competition in the great majority of states.[1] In the late nineteenth and early twentieth centuries the Senate was a bastion of conservatism, something of a "rich man's club," and highly resistant to liberal or progressive sentiment. Since World War II the Senate has been the more liberal half of the Congress on most issues and has been highly responsive

---

This article originally appeared in *The Congress and America's Future,* 2d ed., ed. David B. Truman (Englewood Cliffs, N.J.: Prentice-Hall, Inc., 1973).

[1]The best account of the late nineteenth-century Senate is David Rothman, *Politics and Power: The U.S. Senate, 1869-1901* (Cambridge: Harvard University Press, 1967).

3

to the legislative demands of various marginal voting groups. In turn, this trend plus a high degree of chamber decentralization and good opportunity for media coverage have made the Senate a major breeding ground for presidential candidates.

By contrast, the House in the twentieth century has become more conservative and less subject to competition in the great majority of congressional districts. Thus a second major trend, resulting from the combined effects of safe districts plus the seniority system, has been the *professionalization of the House career*.[2] The "activist political minorities" that are so important for the statewide politics of the Senate (and the presidency) are important for only a few House districts. At least three-quarters of all House districts are relatively "safe" year after year.[3] This lack of effective party competition at the congressional district level has made reelection to the House generally possible. And the twentieth-century emphasis on the seniority system—which was *not* the standard practice in the nineteenth century—has made repeated reelection desirable and indeed necessary for the member who wants to have an impact on what the House does.

THE FORMAL RULES OF THE GAME

Structural Differences Between Houses

The structural differences between the House and Senate can be dealt with briefly. The six-year term for senators removes them somewhat from the pressure of imminent reelection campaigns. The two-year term for representatives means that a member from a relatively competitive district is almost perpetually campaigning. House members from "safe" districts, however, may face serious challenge even less frequently than does the typical senator. The reality is thus one of frequent elections but with little

---

[2]H. D. Price, "The Congressional Career: Then and Now" (1964 working paper for The American Assembly), reprinted in *Congressional Behavior,* ed. Nelson W. Polsby (New York: Random House, 1971). For a more teleological view see Polsby, "The Institutionalization of the U.S. House of Representatives," *ibid.*

[3]For an extensive survey of American experience see Milton C. Cummings, *Congressmen and the Electorate* (New York: Free Press, 1966).

serious competition in the case of most members of the House; for the Senate it is infrequent election but a much higher probability of serious opposition.

The equal representation of states in the Senate makes that body technically unrepresentative of sheer population, but there are very few issues that tend to pit small states as such against the states with a large population. And most major sections of the country include states with both large and small populations. The most concentrated sectional over-representation in the Senate is of the Rocky Mountain West (including the Southwest). The eight mountain states elect 16 senators, but on a population basis are entitled to only 17 of the 435 House members (which tells a lot about why the Senate has been more responsive than the House to silver miners and sheep herders).

The apportionment of House seats among the states has, since 1929, been put on an automatic basis. But the drawing of individual district lines within a state has long been a problem. Incumbent representatives often oppose upsetting established district lines, and state legislatures controlled by one party have opposed changes that might improve the electoral chances of the other party. States gaining an additional House seat have frequently resorted to electing the additional member at large. Opportunities for such vagaries were finally narrowed, however, by the Supreme Court's reapportionment decisions.[4] These still leave some room for judicious gerrymandering, but only within the confines of districts with substantially equal population. Most state legislatures have done a remarkable job of shoring up the electoral base of most incumbents of both parties and thus of narrowing even further the number of close competitive districts.

Processes of Representation

A consequence of the electoral process is that local constituencies—states for the Senate, districts for the House—are provided "representation" through at least three separate processes. First, there is a kind of automatic representation that is roughly achieved by taking almost any individual from a given state or local district. Senator Eastland of Mississippi and

---

[4]For a recent summary see Nelson W. Polsby, ed., *Reapportionment in the 1970's* (Berkeley: University of California Press, 1971).

Harlem's Congressman Rangel take sharply contrasting stands on civil rights and integration, and the chances are that most white Mississippi residents and almost any Harlem Negro would do likewise. On such basic issues a legislator himself is likely to share the basic views of his effective constituency and to be in no need of a poll on the subject.

A second process of representation occurs through the election system itself. On issues where the local constituency is not so overwhelmingly in agreement, or where a legislator gets widely out of line with the grass-roots view, then the electoral process provides a means for a popular test. Theoretically, at least, an incumbent may be defeated by an opponent of the opposite party or in a primary contest. This possibility of dumping one man and replacing him with another remains the ultimate sanction in a democratic system, but it is something of a blunderbuss weapon. Elections are infrequent, at times set by law rather than by the rise and fall of popular issues, and there may be a great many issues but only two candidates.

The possibility of opposition, however, remains a powerful factor in attuning the incumbent to the third process of representation. This is the more subtle process by which constituents can express opinions and exert influence in such a manner that the politically sophisticated legislator can, if he desires, make an estimate of the amount of local backing (in terms of influence, not of counting noses) and adapt his position accordingly. Thus the incumbent can often adjust to changes in the make-up of his constituency, to shifts in the national climate, or to new and urgent demands from individuals or groups that are important to him or to his district.[5] To the extent that the representative can, and is willing to, perform this third type of delicate representation, then the probability of the electorate resorting to the second type (throwing the rascal out) is reduced. But the possibility of defeat remains, and in the case of a major electoral landslide it often falls equally on the just and the unjust.

Each of these processes of representation depends upon a variety of institutional arrangements. Operation of the first form is guaranteed through

---

[5]The first systematic effort to distinguish between alternative "paths" or processes of representation is Warren E. Miller and Donald E. Stokes, "Constituency Influence in Congress," *American Political Science Review* 57 (March 1963): 45-56, reprinted in *Elections and the Political Order,* ed. Angus Campbell et al. (New York: Wiley, 1966).

residence requirements. The sharp contrast between the American emphasis on local residence and the British practice of assigning parliamentary candidates to seats anywhere in the country has often been noted. In point of fact, however, the American practice is largely informal; the Constitution requires only that a member "when elected, be an inhabitant of that state" in which he is chosen. As the nomination of Pierre Salinger for the Senate in California and the election of Robert Kennedy in New York show, this is a nominal requirement. But the informal emphasis on a "local man," who knows, appreciates, and is responsive to the local scene, is still the norm. The customary length of local residence necessary for political acceptance, however, may vary from several generations (in parts of the South) to barely a decade (in southern California or peninsular Florida).

The other two paths of representation, via physical replacement or by bringing about a change of opinion (or at least of vote) by the same incumbent rest upon the use, or possibility of use, of the electoral system. Here again we find a major contrast between the twentieth-century Congress and that of the nineteenth century. Up to the turn of the century the likelihood of electoral turnover was quite high: more states and districts were competitive; party slates were voted on as a whole, with little opportunity for differentiation; and few alternative channels of opinion—such as interest groups—were active in Washington. Since 1900 fewer House districts have been competitive; ballot forms have been changed so as to encourage voting "for the man rather than the party"; and a myriad of groups seek to sway a legislator's vote rather than wait and try to replace him.

The overall pattern of the legislative career is structured by three successive choice points. First, though often ignored, is the willingness of a member to serve out his elected term and seek reelection. Throughout the nineteenth century the greater part of turnover in House members and Senators was not due to electoral defeat, but to voluntary retirement after a term or two, or even resignation without completing one's term.[6] In the

---

[6]Thus in the early nineteenth century barely one-third of the members of the Senate would bother to run for reelection, with roughly equal numbers resigning or quitting at the completion of their term. Concurrently almost 90 percent of the departures from the House were due to resignations or refusal to stand for reelection, rather than to electoral defeat.

twentieth century the attractions of the legislative career have reduced such departures drastically. The second and third winnowing processes, for those desiring to pursue a long-run career, involve renomination by the party and reelection in the November general election. Chronologically the primary election hurdle comes first, but the much greater importance of the general election warrants taking it up first. As we shall see, the primary for most members in most years is a very pale imitation of a contested electoral process.

THE GENERAL ELECTION: SHARED FATES?

What influences the general election vote for House and Senate candidates, and to what extent can they hope to affect either the electoral turnout or direction of the vote in their constituency? These are very large questions, for which isolated cases and casual impressions provide conflicting answers. Over the past decade these questions have been pursued on a systematic basis in regard to House elections by Gerald Kramer,[7] and in a different way by Donald E. Stokes.[8] Both have provided notable perspectives from which to evaluate the extent to which the various candidates on a party ticket are involved in a "shared fate" and what seem to be the most important factors affecting the outcomes. Kramer concentrates on the extent to which the overall congressional vote seems to reflect changes in the performance of the economy. Stokes attempts to disentangle the relative effects of all (unspecified) forces attributable to the individual district, then to common statewide trends, and finally to common nationwide trends.

Again it is useful to consider the baseline of nineteenth-century practice. Down to the 1890s each party printed up a slate of its candidates that the voter had only to take in hand and deposit in the ballot box. On rare occasions some voters might "scratch" the name of one or more party candidates, but the tendency was to generate a "straight" party vote with

---

[7]Gerald Kramer, "Short-Term Fluctuations in U.S. Voting Behavior, 1886-1964," *American Political Science Review* 65 (1971): 131-43.

[8]Donald E. Stokes, "Parties and the Nationalization of Electoral Forces," in *The American Party Systems,* ed. William N. Chambers and Walter Dean Burnham (New York: Oxford University Press, 1967), 182-202.

remarkably little difference in the vote for president, governor, House, state legislator, and so on. Beginning in 1889, however, reform movements succeeded in having a few states adopt the Australian practice of printing up a single official ballot listing all the alternative candidates for each office.[9] This made it much easier for voters to skip back and forth across party lines. Indeed, as more states adopted the reform, many sought to further discourage "straight" party voting by adopting a ballot organized not into columns of candidates arranged by party, but rather into successive blocs of candidates grouped together under the office for which they were running. The full impact of these changes was not evident at first, but over time they facilitated tendencies for many voters to cross party lines, or to vote only for president, or both. The extent to which candidates were indeed linked together in a shared electoral fate was thus markedly reduced. Over time there were obvious incentives for incumbents to cultivate personal appeals and for the parties to promote complex "United Nations" slates of balanced religious and nationality groupings (appealing to the increasingly heterogeneous nature of the twentieth century electorate).

Individual candidates for the House and Senate, whether incumbents or challengers, can seek to influence the size and direction of the vote in many ways. Such efforts may spell the difference between victory and defeat but are still limited to making marginal changes in such massive tendencies as for the presidential vote to far exceed the turnout in nonpresidential election years, or for the electorate to react negatively to an incumbent party in the event of a noticeable downturn of the economy. Political folklore suggests that the Republicans do better in periods of prosperity, with the electorate turning to the Democrats in periods of "bad times." By contrast a rational model of electoral behavior would react symmetrically to the parties, punishing either party's candidates for poor performance of the economy.

ECONOMIC INFLUENCES

For the period 1896-1964 (excepting war years and the 1912 three-party election), Gerald Kramer finds impressive evidence that the share of the

---

[9]For the impact of this on voting behavior see Jerrold G. Rusk, "The Effect of the Australian Ballot Reform on Split Ticket Voting: 1876-1908," *American Political Science Review* 64 (1970): 1220-38.

total two-party vote for candidates of a party does indeed vary quite systematically with the state of the economy. Moreover, his evidence supports the rational-model view that the parties are indeed treated equally, despite the historic association of the GOP with the post-1929 depression. Historical evidence on party turnover of seats for the post-Reconstruction period (say, 1874-1894) suggests that the same process was at work then, but with a much higher proportion of House seats changing hands than in the twentieth century.

Kramer's analysis, which works from objective economic variables (primarily real income, with neither unemployment nor cost-of-living proving very useful) to the congressional vote skips over the customary role of voter attitudes. Detailed attitudinal data are simply not available for the pre-World War II period. Kramer's rational-model approach to the congressional vote can, however, be reconciled with the attitudes-as-predictor approach (associated with the University of Michigan's Survey Research Center) by thinking of his estimates as short-cuts in a somewhat more complex process.

Thus for nonpresidential elections one might visualize the process roughly as indicated in Figure 1. Kramer's estimates simply bypass the unmeasured intervening variable of attitude. The actual causal process might be assumed to operate via the solid arrows (through attitudes) rather than directly across (via the dashed arrow). For the process to work over time democratic theory would suggest inclusion, at the right of the model, of a box for government policy toward the economy, which is influenced—perhaps in anticipation—by the vote and in turn seeks to affect the level of real income. The Nixon administration's adoption of Phase II controls, after a disappointing Republican showing in the 1970 elections, suggests the extent to which both parties have come to accept the logic of some such relationship.

In presidential election years the situation is a bit more complicated. Then electoral turnout increases sharply, especially among independents and voters with weak party loyalties. In this context the specific presidential candidates and their campaign tactics have a substantial impact on the vote for president. Since House and Senate candidates are voted on at the same time and on the same ballot as the president, there is likely to be some presidential "coattail" effect on the vote for Congress. Kramer finds that in mid-term elections some 56 percent of the total variance in the major-party vote could be attributed to the economic variables; in presidential years this

Figure 1. *Shared Fate in Terms of Voting for the House of Representatives: Kramer-Style Model of Economic Influences on Variations in the House Vote, 1896-1964*

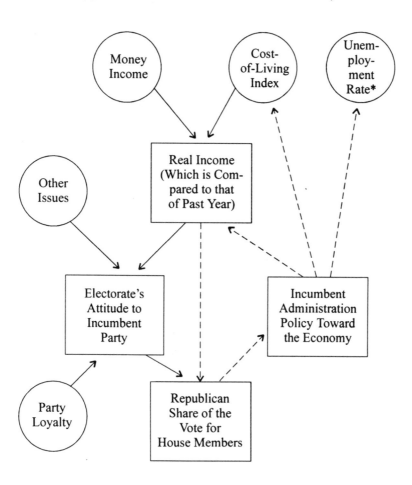

Note: Unemployment rate is not statistically significant in predicting the House vote.

drops to 47 percent, but with an additional 16 percent due to effects of the presidential election.[10]

DISTRICT, STATE, AND NATIONAL TRENDS

Another way of looking at sources of change in the vote for Congress is to attempt to assess the proportion of the total variation that can be attributed to the individual House district, to statewide trends, and finally to a nationwide trend (for the Senate the division would be simply between state effects and nationwide trend, unless one wanted to introduce multistate regions). House districts are neatly "nested" together state by state, and the states are equally neatly nested together within the nation. Donald Stokes has capitalized on this to estimate, within apportionment decades (such as 1952-60), the average relative magnitude of district-level, state-level, and nation-level effects on both turnout and partisan division of the vote. If one is interested in the extent to which congressional candidates can hope to influence their electoral fate, then the relative size of the district-level effects is a very useful piece of information.

For the decades since Reconstruction Table 1 indicates the relative extent of variation in the partisan division of the vote that Stokes attributes to the local district level. The salience of the local district increases sharply from the 1880s to the 1890s (the decade of greatest ballot change), then remains relatively stable through the 1920s. Under the impact of the depression and Roosevelt's New Deal the role of the local district declines sharply in the 1930s (to the same figure as held for the 1880s). There are further modest declines for the 1940s and 1950s. In regard to extent of electoral turnout Stokes' analysis suggests a much simpler picture: local district influence marks a rather steady decline over most of the entire period, with the sharpest drop between the decade of the 1900s and the 1910s.

Stokes' ingenious analysis sheds light on a problem involving two contrasting trends.[11] On the one hand the local constituency should be of

---

[10]Kramer, 140.

[11]For an extension and critique of the Stokes analysis see the article by Richard S. Katz, "Rejoinder to 'Comment' by Donald E. Stokes," *American Political Science Review* 67 (1973): 832-34.

Table 1. *Changes in Magnitude of Local Constituency Influence on Partisan Division of the Vote for House Members, By Decades (Based on Donald Stokes' Calculation of Variance Components*)*

Period Analyzed**	Size of Constituency-Variance Compound
1872-80	26.7
1882-90	21.9
1892-1900	32.1
1902-10	28.1
1912-20	33.2
1922-30	36.5
1932-40	21.9
1942-50	18.7
1952-60	14.0
1962-70	(too much reapportionment to permit comparable analysis)

*See Donald E. Stokes, "Parties and the Nationalization of Electoral Forces," in *The American Party Systems*, ed. William N. Chambers and Walter Dean Burnham (New York: Oxford University Press, 1967), 182-202.

**Within each decade each House district is included if (1) it underwent no redistricting within the decade, and (2) each major party nominated a candidate in each election. Thus most of the South is excluded.

increasing importance because of the weakening of party loyalty and organization, the abandonment of party-supplied ballots, and the use of the primary election with its tendency to encourage members to "paddle their own canoes." On the other hand one might expect the local district to be of less importance *vis-à-vis* the national scene because of the spread of common living conditions (an urban, industrial way of life) and consequent issues, plus the increased importance of the presidency and of such potent national media as radio (in the 1930s) and, more recently, television.

Perhaps the most important limitation of the Stokes analysis is that it does not permit one to distinguish between effects in presidential and mid-term elections. The drop in participation in mid-term elections has developed largely since 1900 and is so regular a feature of twentieth-century elections that it would be useful to consider a specific "presidential effect" that is superimposed on the district, state, and national effects (estimating the "national" effect not due to the presidential campaign from the various mid-term elections). This should reduce the size of the presumed national effect quite substantially, especially for mid-term elections, and permit the identification of a specific presidential effect operative only in presidential election years.

The increased turnout of the electorate in presidential election years makes the partisan division of the vote in such years substantially more variable than in mid-term elections. V. O. Key summarized the reasons for this years ago:

> Explanation of the Administration's loss at midterm must be sought not so much by examining the midterm election itself as by looking at the preceding presidential election. The presidential campaign mobilizes party strength behind the winning presidential candidate and apparently has the secondary effect of capturing some marginal congressional seats, and of holding a few other such seats, for candidates of the President's party. At the midterm the absence of the supportive power of the presidential campaign allows some districts, usually held by the narrowest margin, to sag over the line to the opposition.[12]

Key's analysis has been amply vindicated by Survey Research Center interview data, which Angus Campbell deals with in terms of "surge and decline" of the presidential and mid-term electorates.[13]

In general the mid-term elections offer somewhat less of a hazard to most House and Senate incumbents, since their party membership usually will match that of the majority of party identifiers in their constituency. The exceptions are the members who have been swept in largely because of the added "coattail" effects of a presidential election. Since they are often from

---

[12]V. O. Key, *Politics, Parties, and Pressure Groups*, 4th ed. (New York: Crowell, 1958), 615-16.

[13]Angus Campbell, "Surge and Decline: A Study of Electoral Change," *Public Opinion Quarterly* (Fall 1960), reprinted in *Elections and the Political Order*, ed. Angus Campbell et al. (New York: Wiley, 1966).

the party in a minority locally they are likely to face an up-hill struggle to survive in the more party-oriented mid-term election. Hence the customary twentieth-century tendency for the party capturing the presidency to gain some added strength in Congress in the presidential election only to lose most of the gains in the following mid-term election.

PARTY IDENTIFICATION

Variations in the vote for House members, and analogously for senators, thus reflect a substantial response of the electorate to the state of the economy, plus a variety of less easily identified factors. A portion of this variation is due to forces operating at the district level, another (usually smaller) portion reflects forces common to each state. But a substantial part of the variation, especially in the case of level of turnout, reflects general nationwide trends. The sources of variation, however, do not operate on an otherwise unstructured electorate. Rather, they work to displace the vote from its underlying partisan division.[14] The extent to which there is a substantial corps of loyal Republican and of loyal Democratic voters in a state or district is of crucial importance. "Safe" states and districts are simply a manifestation of a lopsided distribution of party identifiers. The surplus of party loyalists for one or the other party simply put such states or districts beyond the reach of most short-term forces that affect variation in the vote.

It is well known that a majority of the national electorate have some sort of enduring attachment to one or the other major party. Most voters do not have to stop and "decide" every two years which party they are going to favor; they have a standing decision in favor of one or the other. Much the same thing is true of most congressional districts—and used to be the case with a majority of states. The most marked differences in the incidence of close two-party competition are between the state-level Senate contests and the individual congressional district contests. This in turn is due to the

---

[14]The concept of a pure (normalized) party vote is developed by Phillip E. Converse, in Chapter 2 of *Elections and the Political Order*. For its application to Congress see Harvey M. Kabaker, "Estimating the Normal Vote in Congressional Elections," *Midwest Journal of Political Science* 13 (1969): 58-83.

marked increase in the number of competitive states, which reflects the steady erosion of sectionalism in the nation.

Evidence for the change toward greater competition at the state level is available on every side. It is indicated in registration figures, in presidential voting patterns, and in the sharp increase in the number of senators elected by narrow margins. The change in the fundamental geographical basis of partisanship can be seen by comparing the presidential vote of 1900 and 1960: in 1900 there were 18 states in which the Democrats polled less than 40 or more than 60 percent, and only 15 states in which the Democratic percentage of the vote ranged from 45 to 55 percent. In 1960 in contrast, there were 34 states in which the Democratic vote ranged between 45 and 55 percent, and only six states in which it was under 40 or over 60 percent.

Although the presidential vote is somewhat more volatile than voting for Senate or House members, the same trend is clearly evident in regard to Senate elections. Thus of all senators elected in 1960 and 1962, almost half won by margins of less than 55 percent, and over two-thirds won by less than 60 percent. But the various population and economic trends that are working toward producing two-party competition in virtually every state are not producing such competition within the more restricted confines of the individual House district. In most postwar elections less than 100 of the 435 House seats have been won by under 55 percent. The "swing" district, like the highly rational "independent" voter, is an exception to the rule and not the usual thing. Electoral turnover has been limited largely to this political "no-man's land." Indeed, Professor Charles O. Jones, in a detailed study of party turnover in the twentieth-century House of Representatives, points out that the number of House districts experiencing change of party control has gradually decreased for half a century.[15]

The "safe" one-party House seats are to be found in every part of the country, including the big, industrialized states that are very closely balanced at the statewide level. Thus in 1962 Pennsylvania voters reelected Senator Joseph Clark with 51.2 percent of the vote. But at the same election the same voters elected 23 of the 27 Pennsylvania congressmen by margins

---

[15]Charles O. Jones, "Inter-Party Competition for Congressional Seats," *Western Political Quarterly* 17 (1964): 461-76. By my count the proportion of House districts changing in party control in the decades prior to the 1896 realignment was roughly twice as much as for the decades after 1896.

of greater than 10 percent. Much the same thing holds for New York or Illinois or any of the large states. Thus Figure 2 compares the margin of House and Senate victories in the eight most populous states, which elect all told almost half of the House (211 of 435 seats) and which generally dominate the electoral college. There are roughly as many "safe" districts in these eight competitive states as in the 11 states of the South!

That the ordinary tides of political change lap only into relatively competitive states and districts has been amply demonstrated for both House and Senate by V. O. Key.[16] In areas where the minority party lacks a substantial number of partisan supporters, even the most vigorous efforts by the minority party's nominees are generally unavailing. In the absence of a major error by the incumbents, such challengers just do not have the ordinary baseline of partisan support from which to work that a candidate has in a competitive district and that is necessary for a chance to win. What needs to be emphasized here is both the increasing number of statewide electorates that are becoming susceptible to party change, and the small—and dwindling—number of competitive House districts. These changes in the incidence of competition, in turn, have major consequences for the respective chambers. Close party competition in the House may be increasingly limited to the handful of "swing" districts plus those districts where an incumbent has retired or died. Incumbents have found it increasingly easy to win reelection so long as they make a good impression back home and do not become involved in scandal (such as financial irregularities, excessive drinking in public, or highly publicized marital problems). And for most members, being renominated poses even less of a problem than does the general election.

MAKING PARTY NOMINATIONS: THE DIRECT PRIMARY

Adoption of Primary

Nomination by primary election is a peculiarly American phenomenon. Just as the delegate convention had replaced the old practice of nomination by legislative caucus as a more direct and more democratic procedure, so

---

[16]See the chapter on congressional elections in the fourth or fifth editions of *Politics, Parties, and Pressure Groups* (New York: Crowell).

Figure 2. *Party Competition in the Eight Most Populous States: Percentage Democratic for House Candidates in 1962 and for all Senate Candidates, 1958-62 (Includes New York, California, Pennsylvania, Illinois, Ohio, Texas, Michigan, and New Jersey)*

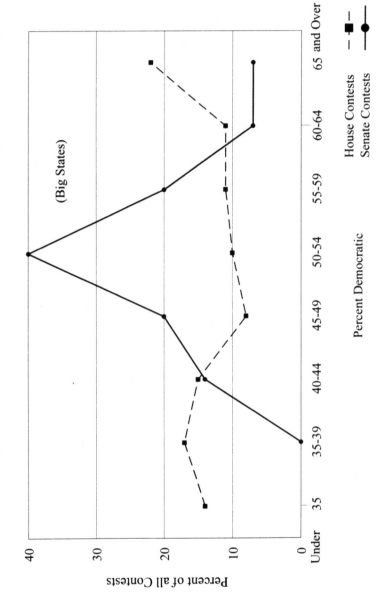

the same reasons led to the primary election replacing the convention. The holding of statewide primaries spread rapidly throughout the South during the decade of the 1890s and was adopted by many northern and western states, beginning with Wisconsin in 1903. By 1960 every state had some sort of primary election system, although a few still make some statewide nominations by convention. But there has been some tendency since World War II for primary states with complex ethnic or nationality mixes to adopt a preprimary convention that can endorse a ticket—usually a "balanced" one—in the party primary.

At the turn of the century two major factors combined to generate unusual enthusiasm for the adoption of the primary and for the related issue of direct election of senators. On the one hand, there was widespread and in many cases justifiable dissatisfaction with the manipulation and control of conventions (and state legislatures) by patronage-based bosses and by various special interests. It was a bit optimistic to hope that a shift to nomination by primaries would remove entirely the influence of party bosses or special interests, but it did change the rules of the game. This change reduced the advantages of some types of candidates and some sorts of interests while improving the position of other candidates and other interests.

The abuses of conventions and of legislative choice of senators were most marked in one-party areas where the general election contest did not constitute a restraining influence. The second factor behind the rapid spread of the primary was the sharp decline in general election competition that occurred in the 1890s. By 1900 so much of the country was one-party Democratic or one-party Republican that if people were to be provided a meaningful vote between rivals it would have to be in the primary. In the South the Negro had been finally removed as a political factor and the Republican party reduced to a nullity. In much of the North the nomination of William Jennings Bryan in 1896 had brought catastrophe to the Democrats. Hence the primary afforded a means of having at least some sort of election contest, and this seemed all the more important since the decline of general election competition severely lessened the restraints on the potential abuses of the largely unregulated convention process. As E. E. Schattschneider has noted, in the period prior to 1896 "the two major parties were able to compete on remarkably even terms throughout the country." As he puts it:

Thus the crisis of 1896 destroyed the balance of the party system. In 1892 there were thirty-six states in which a competitive party situation existed. By 1904 there remained only six states in which the parties were evenly matched, while there were twenty-nine states in which the parties were so unbalanced that the situation could no longer be described as competitive.[17]

Under such circumstances the nomination became, for all practical purposes, the decisive step in the electoral contest in most states.

By and large the primary has proved to be a poor substitute for general election competition, but in the absence of such competition the primary doubtless has substantial advantages over the convention system. The very flexibility of the primary system, however, seems to have worked so as to further weaken the local minority party. Voters and candidates who might have helped to develop the opposition party instead tended to register and to enter politics in the ranks of the dominant majority. And within the majority party lines were fluid, participation was less than in general elections, and incumbents could usually count on reelection. Except in states with sharp factional cleavage, there was no continuing base of support or group of organizers to advance candidates to challenge the incumbent.[18]

Local Emphasis of Primaries

For congressmen and senators the operation of the primary has tended to emphasize the highly decentralized nature of the American party system. At the nominating stage of the process the national party hardly exists. Rather it provides a label that automatically goes to any and all those local candidates who happen to win in the party's local primaries. The candidate may win solely because of his name or because he vigorously opposes the national party on some major local issue, such as busing in the South. Thus

---

[17]E. E. Schattschneider, "United States: The Functional Approach to Party Government," in *Modern Political Parties,* ed. Sigmund Neumann (Chicago: University of Chicago Press, 1956), 203.

[18]The classic account of the difference that the lack of a continuing, organized corps of voters and candidates makes is still Chapter 14 of V. O. Key, *Southern Politics* (New York: Knopf, 1949).

in each state and in most congressional districts the party nomination is up for grabs. Or at least it is when the incumbent is not a candidate for renomination.

The tendency for incumbents to win renomination is a tribute both to the material advantages that accrue to the incumbent and to the skill with which most incumbents work to keep their local fences mended. Charles L. Clapp, summarizing a series of round-table sessions held with both Republican and Democratic members, put the matter this way:

> Although members of Congress are inclined to talk about reelection campaigns in terms of the problems involved, they agree that as incumbents they possess extraordinary advantages over their opponents. There is a tendency to believe that, aside from isolated instances where an overriding issue is present, there is little excuse for defeat.[19]

But many members cultivate their constituencies, even in the nonelection year, as if the best way to avoid possible defeat were to scare off any potential competition. And House members have the added decennial threat of changed district boundaries, or even having two incumbents thrown into the same district.

In an analysis of the 1968 primaries for the 302 House seats outside the South and border states Frank Sorauf found that in all but 28 districts the incumbent was running for reelection.[20] Only 87 of the 274 incumbents faced any primary competition at all, and there were only 23 instances (less than 10 percent) where the winner's margin was less than two to one. For the out-party nomination and where an incumbent had retired, competition was more common but still limited. Even in the major party primaries lacking an incumbent, in more than half there was no contest at all. As Sorauf concludes, "the democratic hopes behind the direct primary falter on the lack of competition and low voter turnout."[21]

Sociologists have found it useful to distinguish between educational systems that operate along lines of sponsored mobility (such as the British

---

[19]Charles L. Clapp, *The Congressman: His Work as He Sees It* (Washington: Brookings Institution, 1963), 330.

[20]Frank Sorauf, *Party Politics in America,* 2d ed. (Boston: Little, Brown, 1972), 227.

[21]*Ibid.,* 226.

preparatory schools for the upper classes) as contrasted with a more open system of contest mobility (such as American public schools and low-tuition state universities). Much the same distinction can be made in regard to party nominating systems—British parties sponsor candidates and assign them constituencies in order to bring them into the national political scene. In American parties the local primary is generally an open contest to be won by a local candidate campaigning on issues of local concern.

The most difficult problem for a president seeking to influence the outcome of a primary is where an anti-administration incumbent is faced by a challenger. Aided by wartime enthusiasm, Woodrow Wilson was successful in intervening in several southern primaries in 1918. But Franklin D. Roosevelt was generally unsuccessful in his 1938 "purge" efforts, which were undertaken without much advance planning.[22] Except in unusual circumstances, it would appear that national party leaders are more likely to be effective by quietly searching out a strong local candidate or a national figure with a local connection, than by public denunciation of the incumbent. Campaign contributors and assorted technicians (media specialists and political pollsters) can be steered in the direction of a favored contender.

Like the common cold, a primary is seldom fatal but it is almost always an unpleasant disruption. Time, funds, and energy that could otherwise be channeled in other directions have to be diverted to the local scene. Small wonder that most legislators find it advantageous to cultivate the home state or district on a continuous basis, especially in nonelection years, in the hope of deterring primary opposition. In some states and in a good many House districts the same tactic can be used to reduce somewhat the risks of the general election.

Prior political experience and an existing base of support are vital in capturing initial nomination to the House, and a virtual necessity in running for the Senate. Thus House nominations often go to members of a state legislature or of local government, especially in the case of the local

---

[22]On presidential intervention in primaries see Austin Ranney and Willmore Kendall, *Democracy and the American Party System* (New York: Harcourt, Brace and World, 1956), 286-89; and William Riker, *Democracy in the United States* (New York: Macmillan, 1953), 285-93. By contrast, presidential involvement in mid-term elections, in November, has come to be both accepted and expected.

majority party. The minority party's nomination, often regarded as a useless honor, is more easily captured by a political neophyte. In turn, the members of the House constitute the single largest source of successful Senate candidates—a point of some dismay to many House leaders. In his study of the 180 members serving in the Senate from 1947 to 1957 D. R. Matthews found that almost half had been elected to some public office prior to reaching age 30 and that less than 10 percent came to the Senate without previously holding some public office.[23] He found the most frequent stepping stones to the Senate to be (in decreasing order of importance): House of Representatives, governorship, state or federal administrative office, and law-enforcement posts. In contrast to the nineteenth century, direct movement from state legislature to the Senate occurs for barely one in 10 senators.

Nominations are thus generally on a do-it-yourself basis with the incumbent enjoying substantial advantages. Most candidates and most voters do not consider the nomination to be a national matter in which local preferences receive some consideration, but rather as primarily local matters in which any attempt at national intervention, or even outside comment by mass media, may backfire. Thus a popular president (or presidential candidate) may lend great strength to his party's entire ticket in November, but he finds it extraordinarily difficult to influence the primaries that determine the make-up of the remainder of that ticket. One of the few means available is by steering major campaign contributors to favored incumbents or—a more risky move—to favored challengers in the party primaries.

CAMPAIGN FINANCE: THE HIGH COST OF CANDIDACY

"It costs too much to run for office." On this incumbents and challengers, Republicans and Democrats all agree. In most parts of the country it does cost a great deal to wage an effective campaign for the House or Senate. Moreover, most of the money has to be raised locally by the candidate and his supporters. The national parties can supply only limited funds plus some research materials and advice to their nominees—and

---

[23]Donald R. Matthews, *U.S. Senators and Their World* (Chapel Hill: University of North Carolina Press, 1960), 50-55.

sometimes they may furnish nothing more than a telegram of congratulations.

In a few states, such as heavily industrialized Ohio or Michigan, the state Republican organization may carry out a "united fund" type of drive for the benefit of the entire party ticket. The Democrats, lacking a natural financial base such as the business community, are less likely to be able to carry out such a coordinated fundraising operation. Except for areas with unusually active labor unions, as in Michigan, or a powerful city organization, as in Chicago, Democratic nominees are likely to have to scrounge for funds on their own. The local emphasis on fundraising thus constitutes another decentralizing feature of the electoral process.

Amounts

Precise accounts of the amounts spent in campaigns are hard to come by. Because of unrealistic state and federal limits, many candidates have made it a point not to know in detail how much is being spent in their behalf. But the general order of magnitude is well known. In a large state, expenditure of over a million dollars in a Senate race is regarded as regrettable but necessary. Costs for a House campaign vary widely. An incumbent from a safe district may need only to pay his filing fee, but in a closely contested urban district a figure of from fifty to one hundred thousand dollars is not unusual. Much of course depends upon the amount of use made of television and whether the House candidate conducts a separate campaign or the party runs a joint one.

The increasing cost of campaigning and the paucity of national party assistance probably work to the advantage of the incumbent and may mean better access for those local interests that do help foot the bill. In 1962 James A. Michener, the well-known novelist, waged a determined but unsuccessful campaign in a strong Republican district north of Philadelphia. He notes:

> I have come upon quite a few facts I have [sic] not known before. The incumbent has an overwhelming advantage. . . . He mails letters free. You pay for yours. For him to send a piece of literature to each family costs about $6,000 paid for by the taxpayers. You cough up your own $6,000 in cash.

He has at his command a staff of about five secretaries and helpers with a total yearly salary of around $45,000 paid for by the taxpayers. You find one girl and pay her yourself.[24]

Every two years a summary and analysis of major campaign contributions is prepared by the Citizens' Research Foundation. The sums reported in presidential election contests are astronomical, and spirited mid-term House or Senate contests often involve breathtaking amounts. Thus in 1970 New York Congressman Richard Ottinger ran for the Senate. He lost, but not for lack of funds or family enthusiasm, the family contributions to his campaign having amounted to some 3.9 million dollars (a figure not too far behind that reported for the family of Governor Nelson Rockefeller). Looking just at unsuccessful bids for Congress in 1970 one runs across the following examples of the direct family contributions to the costs of candidacy:[25]

Candidate	Family Contribution	Election (all 1970)
A. J. Donahue (Conn.)	$699,700	Lost Senate primary
Norton Simon (Calif.)	1,880,000	Lost Senate primary
F. H. Schultz (Fla.)	309,000	Lost Senate primary
H. M. Metzenbaum (Ohio)	507,500	Lost Senate election
Karen Burstein (N.Y.)	104,000	Defeated for House
L. Curtis (Mass.)	27,500	Defeated for House
P. J. Hillings (Calif.)	43,883	Defeated for House
D. J. Houton (Mass.)	30,130	Defeated for House
W. F. McCall, Jr. (Calif.)	40,999	Defeated for House
Jennifer Smith (N.Y.)	183,000	Defeated for House
P. J. Sprague (N.Y.)	240,425	Defeated for House
E. J. Stack (Fla.)	38,450	Defeated for House
W. D. Weeks (Mass.)	64,500	Defeated for House

---

[24]Quoted in Michael J. Kirwan, *How to Succeed in Politics* (New York: Macfadden Books, 1964), 20. For the 1970s, of course, most of these figures would have to be almost doubled.

[25]The 1970 report is summarized in *The New York Times*, April 19, 1972, p. 28.

Clearly money alone does not guarantee success, but it can be a very great advantage.[26]

SOURCES

Since around 1900 both state and federal governments have made sporadic efforts at limiting, or at least making public, amounts and sources of campaign spending. Direct contributions by corporations or by labor unions have been prohibited, but efforts at limiting total amount of spending or total individual contributions have had so many loopholes as to be useless (in fact, their chief effect has probably been to reduce public awareness of the facts, which have been muddied by the need for multiple letterhead committees that receive multiple checks from an individual or family).[27] Finally, in 1972 Congress passed a new Federal Election Campaign Practices Act which plugs many of the loopholes; imposes limits on what a candidate and his family can contribute and on total spending for radio, television, and other communications media, and seeks to establish an extensive system for reporting contributions and expenditures.[28] Only time and experience will prove whether the new measure will survive possible amendment, probable court tests, and administrative difficulties of compliance.

When measured against the magnitude of the task, the very limited amounts that can be made available to candidates (usually with emphasis on incumbents) by the Republican and Democratic campaign committees of

---

[26]Successful Senate candidate John Tunney (California) reported family contributions of $123,475. Representative James H. Scheuer reported family contributions of $126,440 in his campaign for reelection. The 1970 championship, both for total expenditure and for family contribution, went to Nelson Rockefeller for his successful reelection campaign as governor. According to the foundation analysis it cost around $8 million, with some $5 million coming from various Rockefellers.

[27]A classic case in the mobilization of wealth, even in a state with a rather strict campaign finance law, was John F. Kennedy's successful 1952 campaign for the Senate. See H. D. Price, "Campaign Finance in Massachusetts in 1952," *Public Policy* 6 (1955): 25-46.

[28]See *Congressional Quarterly Almanac,* 1971, for the debate, and 1972 for final enactment.

the House and Senate pale into relative insignificance. Even these amounts are doled out in each party by independent House and Senate campaign committees, thus reenforcing the natural decentralizing tendencies of the American electoral system. Organized labor usually picks up part of the tab for many Democrats—plus an occasional liberal Republican. But probably the most potent centralizing tendency would be the adoption of a system of federal underwriting of at least some of the costs, especially of presidential contests. Senator Russell Long's proposal to permit each taxpayer to earmark a one-dollar tax deduction to be channeled to the party of his choice was adopted by Congress, but then repealed before it could go into effect. The 1972 law includes such a provision, but only to take effect *after* the 1972 election (for which the Republicans saw themselves as being in a much better financial position than the debt-ridden, out-of-power Democrats). And the overall difficulty of adequately yet equitably financing congressional elections is increased by the substantial—and growing—range of resources available to incumbent members of both House and Senate. Not least of these is the member's activities on behalf of individual constituents.

CARE AND FEEDING OF CONSTITUENTS: THE LEGISLATOR AS OMBUDSMAN

A visitor to the House or Senate office buildings is likely to be impressed by the clatter of electric typewriters, the whir of mimeograph machines, and the stacks of outgoing mail. Most of this blur of activity has little or nothing to do with pending legislation or public policy, but a great deal to do with the reelection possibilities of the members of the House and Senate. Prompt attention to mail, careful follow-up on individual "case" work, and maximum cultivation of district (or state) contacts and media add to the secret weapons by which the modern incumbent hopes to remain in office.

Individual Casework

Several Scandinavian countries have a special official, the *Ombudsman,* who receives complaints and tries to help the average citizen in his contacts with the bureaucracy. But a general complaint bureau is one agency that the New Deal did not get around to establishing. In its stead the United States has 535 legislators who serve—with amazing effectiveness—as "ombudsmen" for their local constituents. As various federal agencies came to have more and more complicated contacts with individual citizens, it was inevitable that some bureaucratic errors would be made and that many people would not know what to do about a missing Social Security check or getting an emergency furlough for a serviceman overseas. The simple solution was to "write your congressman" and hope he could help. Within a generation the flow of requests for help or advice has grown from a tiny trickle into a massive daily tide of mail. And in the process modern senators and congressmen have come to perform functions—and enjoy a continued tenure—undreamed of by their nineteenth-century predecessors.

In most congressional offices there are secretaries who specialize in the various types of "case work" and know the appropriate liaison personnel in the various downtown departments. On the Senate side the volume of work for a single senator may be so great that various secretaries will deal exclusively with cases involving veterans' affairs, or Social Security, or the Department of Defense. This provides a helpful function for the citizen and also can give the legislator some rough idea of some of the problem areas and weak spots of bureaucratic operation. And its political value is beyond question. It was providing assistance in an hour of need that helped cement the immigrant's loyalty to the big-city machines of bygone years. In an updated, white-collar sort of way, today's legislators perform a similar—but much more technical—function. And it is appreciated.

Not all "cases" are small matters. There are "big" problems too, involving disposition of federal land or property, status of urban renewal requests, the location of proposed projects and installations, complex contract negotiations, and all the rest of the contacts between federal agencies and local citizens, local business firms, or even local governmental units. Here again the assistance of the local congressman or senator may be of vital importance. But the dividing line between proper and improper involvement is hard to define, and problems of "conflict of interest" may arise. But in general the level of congressional ethics, despite occasional lapses, seems to be far above that of most state legislatures. And it may not be much below that of the federal bureaucracy or the world of private business.

28

Promoting the Economy

Since World War II congressmen and senators have also taken on an added role in promoting the growth of the local economy. They are expected to do everything within their power to oppose any move that would destroy local employment or buying power, whether the closing of an ancient naval ropewalk or the curtailing of an obsolescent navy yard. In an age when the federal government is heavily involved in spending not only for defense but also for research and natural resource development, the legislator's local prestige may rise or fall with the curve of federal investment and spending in his state or district. And the member who can land a major plum—such as the NASA Headquarters that went to Houston, Texas—is likely to be regarded as a civic benefactor and local hero.

Finally, a member's name and good works need to be made known to his constituents. Brief radio or television reports may be taped (at cost) and sent to local stations for broadcast, except during campaigns, as a public service. The great majority of members put out some sort of newsletter, and some send out periodic questionnaires. Special letters of congratulations may go to all graduating high school seniors or to newly wed couples. Many members maintain a year-round office in the district or home state. With the increased length of congressional sessions frequent trips home become even more important. Once Congress adjourns, the members from thinly populated areas may cover the local byways in a mobile trailer office, or in a small airplane. As the late Michael J. Kirwan, a chairman of the Democratic Congressional Campaign Committee, once put it: "No Congressman who gets elected and who minds his business should ever be beaten. Everything is there for him to use if he'll only keep his nose to the grindstone and use what is offered."[29]

CONCLUSION: ELECTORAL CHANGE AND INSTITUTIONAL ADAPTATION

What will the impact of the electoral process be on the House and Senate in the years ahead? For the short run "more of the same" is often the safest prediction. But in an important way the question begs the point, since

---

[29]Kirwan, 20.

we have no very sure idea of what the future holds for American political parties and electoral behavior. Looking at the broad sweep of American history it is obvious that major changes in the party system or electoral process have usually had very substantial effects on Congress. But it is sobering to notice that most of the more important effects were unintended and indeed were often not perceived by the major political figures of the day.

The last major change in the electoral base of the House of Representatives came in the 1890s with the triple impact of the emergence of the solid (lily-white) South, adoption of ballot and registration reforms, and massive voter realignment triggered by the Bryan campaign of 1896. All three changes worked strongly to the advantage of incumbents and rapidly produced a crop of veteran legislators who tended to think in terms of decades rather than years. Members with long service wanted their experience recognized and were unwilling to have all committee posts and chairmanships up for grabs every two years as had been the nineteenth-century practice. Discontent over Speaker Joseph Cannon gave the Democrats an added excuse to take the power of committee appointment away from the Speaker when they took over the House in 1911. Subsequently the respective party committees on committees proved unable to resist the demands for respecting seniority of committee service. By roughly 1920 the "modern" House had taken shape: the Speakership had been reduced to a marginal role, the Appropriations Committee had been expanded and strengthened, average terms of prior service were higher and percent freshmen members was lower than at any time in the nineteenth century, and both parties were making committee appointments with scrupulous care for seniority. Except for physical change—two new House office buildings—remarkably little has changed over the past 50 years.

The role that the House has carved out for itself since 1920 may not be ideal, but it will not be easy to change. If the Depression and New Deal could make no lasting impact on the functioning of the House, one hesitates to predict sweeping changes from a modicum of reapportionment, or from the New Politics.[30] A few members—like Brooklyn's Emanuel Celler—may fall by the wayside, but the overall distribution of party support is such that

---

[30]Perhaps the single most likely change for the House is a continued increase in the number of women elected.

most House districts will remain relatively "safe" so long as we have Republicans and Democrats. The increased threat of primary opposition may force incumbents into closer attention to casework or more frequent trips home. It seems unlikely that it can convert House members—of whom we have 435—into the modern senatorial mould of televised public-figure, fearless committee-investigator, and activist issue-agitator. For most members of the House the alternative is between anonymous, specialized attention to committee detail and the possible lure of running for the Senate or other high-visibility office.

In contrast to the House, the "greening" of the Senate has been remarkable. Recent political trends have been reflected much more rapidly there, and senators with an eye on the White House (a numerous band) sometimes have to compete in anticipation of potential trends. The change in Senate style is all the more remarkable given the absence of any major formal changes in the position of the Senate in the past half century. To a substantial degree modern senators seem to be making a virtue of the necessity imposed on them by the shift to direct election, in statewide contests, with a direct primary for nominations. This seems to force most senators into the mainstream of American politics in a way that lopsided House elections do not encourage.

The advantages of using the Senate and its committees as a forum for publicizing issues—and senators—is not entirely new. But it reflects a sharp change from pre-World War I days when major investigations were more often relegated to presidential commissions, and congressional committees met with little or no press coverage. The modern pattern began to emerge in the 1920s, with Senator Tom Walsh's investigation of the Teapot Dome scandal as the most spectacular example. This public-oriented style was well suited to Republican Progressives, many of whom migrated to the Senate after failing to bring the House around to their way of thinking. And it was expanded on in the 1930s by men like Robert Wagner, Bob LaFollette, Jr., and Gerald P. Nye. But it was with the arrival of television—first explored by Estes Kefauver and then by Joseph McCarthy—that senators could begin to put it all together.

What results from the combination of close competitive statewide elections, the existence of many real and some imagined public issues, and the availability of mass media to cover as many subcommittees as the senators can make look exciting? From one point of view it is merely senatorial self-interest, in pursuit of publicity to assist in reelection or in a drive for the presidency. But, as in "The Fable of the Bees," the pursuit of self-interest may be channeled so as to promote the common good. Or, to turn the matter around, in pursuing public issues modern senators have a great deal to gain. The same cannot be said for the current House. There the pursuit of self-interest—and of the public good—is defined in a less spectacular but perhaps no less real way.

Chapter 2

The Congressional Career Then and Now

A TALE OF TWO TEXANS

At one time or another tens of thousands of Americans must think, at least fleetingly, of what it would be like to be a United States senator or representative. To most the idea of a legislative career is not serious but passes as a sort of Walter Mitty daydream. To others, however, the ambition takes root, or perhaps the actual opportunity may loom on the not too distant horizon. To young Sam Rayburn the urge to become a congressman came at age 13 after he listened to a spellbinding speech by Joseph Weldon Bailey, the Texas senator and one-time House minority leader. To Pierre Salinger the opportunity to become a senator from California inspired the ambition.

Joseph Weldon Bailey, Sam Rayburn, and Pierre Salinger represent not merely different types of political careers but also three quite different phases of American politics. The Congress of the 1960s is a vastly different institution from the days of the nineteenth century, as can readily be seen from the differences in the structure of a legislative career. The changes have been sharpest in regard to the House, as is evident from a quick comparison of the careers of Sam Rayburn and the hero of his youth, Congressman (later Senator) Bailey.

Joseph Weldon Bailey entered the House in 1893, one of 135 freshmen members (in the following Congress there were 165 freshmen). The

---

This article originally appeared in *Congressional Behavior,* ed. Nelson W. Polsby (New York: Random House, 1971), 14-27.

Democrats were in the majority, as they had been in the previous Congress, but were engaged in a complex struggle over the Speakership. When William Springer's Illinois delegation found themselves unable to put Springer across, they swung their weight to Carlisle of Georgia, who was elected. Carlisle named Springer to be chairman of the Ways and Means Committee. Bailey, who had backed the wrong candidate, ended up on the Judiciary Committee, but young William Jennings Bryan, a Springer protégé, got a coveted seat on Ways and Means.

To make a long story short, in 1894 Bailey was reelected. Bryan, defeated in his bid for the Senate in 1894, captured the Democratic nomination for president in 1896, but lost under circumstances that further reduced the number of Democrats in Congress. The reduced Democratic contingent in the House turned to Bailey, then starting his third term, as their candidate for Speaker in 1897. Bailey was again his party's leader in the 1899-1900 sessions, after which he was elected to the Senate, where he served until 1913. Had he remained in the House and continued as Democratic leader, he would have been in line for the Speakership in 1911.

Sam Rayburn's 25 continuous terms in the House represent the twentieth-century pattern of legislative leadership, just as Bailey's rapid rise, committee shifts, and switch to the Senate are typical of the nineteenth century. The general patterns of "Mr. Sam's" career are well known, but it is instructive to look at some of the less obvious turning points and some of the roads not taken. Rayburn ran for the Texas legislature in 1906 and was elected at the age of 24. The great issue of the day was prohibition, and Rayburn characteristically moved to a compromise position in support of "local option." Rayburn, who had rapidly won a reputation for fairness and dependability, was elected to a third term in 1910 and was determined to go after the Speakership. After a long and complex struggle, Rayburn, who had the support of the then Senator Bailey, won the post—on the sixty-seventh ballot. (In Georgia young Carl Vinson—who later served for 50 years in Congress—was serving as speaker of the Georgia Assembly.) As Speaker of the legislature, Rayburn was in an excellent position to bid for such statewide office as attorney general, a stepping stone to the governorship. But Texas was, in 1910, gaining two House seats, and the incumbent from what had been Rayburn's district was retiring to run against Bailey for the Senate.

Rayburn's bid for a seat in Congress was thus eased, both by reapportionment and by his predecessor's urge for "promotion" to the Senate. Still, there were eight candidates, and Rayburn (who had bought a Model T Ford for campaigning) won with only 23.4 percent of the votes. He polled 4,983 votes, while his top two rivals received 4,493 and 4,365. When he arrived in Washington in 1913, John N. Garner, the Texas member of the Ways and Means Committee, helped to get him a reasonably good committee assignment, on the Commerce Committee. Garner, who had already served 10 years, was eying the House Speakership, an ambition it was to take him ten more years to reach.

Rayburn faced primary opposition in his first six reelection campaigns and was occasionally to face determined opponents even after becoming the Democratic leader of the House. But he maintained an effective campaign organization and kept in close touch with his district. Rayburn's progress toward the top in the House, however, was to depend in part on the career aspirations of his predecessors. Thus, on the Commerce Committee, Alben Barkley of Kentucky was immediately ahead of Rayburn—had Barkley remained in the House and on the committee, Rayburn would have remained the second-ranking Democrat during the 1930s, and for long thereafter (Barkley died in 1956). Fortunately for Rayburn, Barkley made the switch to the Senate in 1926. Still, the top ranks of the Democratic leadership consisted of his fellow Texan, John Garner, and such other figures as Rainey of Illinois, Bankhead of Alabama, O'Connor of New York, and Byrns of Tennessee. Garner, elected Speaker in 1931, left the House for the vice-presidency in 1933, and was succeeded by Rainey, who had been his floor leader. But Rainey died shortly thereafter, and Rayburn made his move for the Speakership. He was, however, defeated by Byrns, who had been majority floor leader under Rainey. In 1936, Byrns died. His floor leader was John Bankhead, who was in line for the Speakership. Rayburn, sensitive to the apparent succession pattern, did not challenge Bankhead but sought the floor-leader post, which he won in January 1937. When Speaker Bankhead died in 1940, Rayburn moved up to the Speakership, and John McCormack of Massachusetts, a key supporter of Rayburn's, became the new floor leader (and heir apparent).

Rayburn's accomplishments—and his longevity—were exceptional, but in many other respects his career illustrates the crucial turning points in any modern House career. He had the advantages of entering politics early, rising rapidly, and reaching the House by the age of 30. He came from a one-party district, survived subsequent primary contests, and managed to avoid any damaging redistricting or at-large elections. He resisted temptations to seek state office or switch to the Senate. Early arrival plus sheer survival, physical and political, brought him to the chairmanship of his committee. Because he was acceptable to most of his colleagues and the administration, he was in a position to try for the leadership. That he reached the top was due in large part to his skill, persistence, and stamina. But it also was due to the fact that Barkley and Garner were elected to other offices, and that Rainey, Byrns, and Bankhead did not long survive their elevation to the Speakership. In the two decades between Bailey's first election to the House (1892) and Rayburn's (1912) the whole pattern of a House career had drastically changed. See Figure 1.

The structure of the legislative career and the relationship between the two houses on Capitol Hill are largely the result of changes that occurred in the late nineteenth and early twentieth centuries. Throughout most of the nineteenth century service in the House was likely to be a matter of one or, at most, a few terms. Turnover of House membership ranged from 30 to over 60 percent at *every* election, and the average number of terms of prior service represented by a new House generally ranged from one term (or even less) to one and a half terms. The Congress elected in 1900 was the *first* in American history in which new members constituted less than 30 percent of the membership, and it was also the first in which the average of prior service was more than two terms. This, of course, is vastly different from the twentieth-century pattern.

Up until the 1890s only a handful of men had pursued substantial lifetime careers within the House, and they were often the occasion for puzzled comment. Committee chairmen, minority leaders, and even Speakers of the House would leap at the chance to leave that body and become freshmen senators (or sometimes governors). Power within the late nineteenth-century House was highly fluid. Not only was there high turnover of members, there was also frequent alternation of party control. Since relatively few members had substantial seniority, there was no real seniority influence to buck. All committee appointments, both for majority and minority members, as well as the designation of chairmen, were up to the winning candidate for Speaker.

All in all the nineteenth-century House was vastly different from its modern counterpart. In many respects the pre-1900 House was similar to the average current state Assembly: It was a part-time body (in session perhaps nine months out of 24, rather than nine out of 12), with a high degree of membership turnover, with sharp fights for party leadership, and with the

Figure 1. *Seniority and Turnover in the House: Comparison of Number of Members Serving First Term with Number Serving Fifth or Higher Terms, 1893-1899 and 1953-1963*

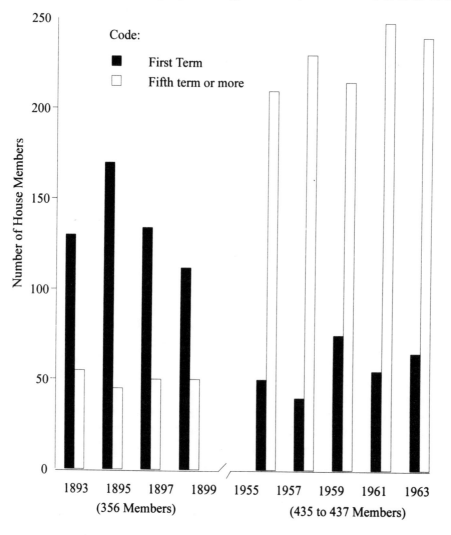

leaders in a position to make all committee appointments and name committee chairmen. The nineteenth-century House was even physically different from that of more recent decades: Members sat at individual desks (rather than on the modern benches), which were often bedecked with flowers, traditionally wore their hats in the chamber (until the 1830s), and were permitted to smoke (until the 1870s).

Lengthy and powerful speeches were still common in the House into the 1890s when Reed's speech on the Wilson tariff bill ran to 15,000 words and required two hours. William Wilson's reply for the Democrats so elated them that they hoisted him onto their shoulders and carried him triumphantly from the chamber. Members often used bitter and outrageous language, scathing ridicule, and sarcasm. Outbreaks of physical violence were not infrequent, and guns and knives were on occasion carried into the chamber.

Constituents were a problem, then as now, but in different ways. There was little mail, and very little departmental "case" work. But members were plagued with continuous demands for government appointments (of which there were many, even after the beginning of civil service in 1883), for local postmasterships (of which there were a vast number, many part time), and for special pension bills (which became something of a national scandal). If modern legislators fret over the heavy mail and case work—most of which can be handled by the member's staff—they can be thankful for the lessened concern with pensions, rural postmasters, and the whole array of government jobs.

Anyone accustomed to the importance of seniority and the extent of stability and specialization in the modern House is apt to find the nineteenth-century House difficult to understand. And yet the key to the development and maintenance of the modern pattern is to be found in the changes that destroyed the old system and laid the groundwork for the modern, professionalized legislative career. By and large these changes have been sharper for the House than for the Senate, but it is important to keep in mind the relations between the two bodies and between the two careers of representative and senator.

Service in the Senate was highly prized, and after the 1820s it was generally regarded as preferable to *any* position in the House, including the speakership. Henry Clay was only the first Speaker to move to the Senate; he was followed by James G. Blaine, John G. Carlisle, Charles F. Crisp, and Frederick H. Gillett. And several minority leaders who did not serve as

Speakers also shifted to the Senate: Joseph W. Bailey, John Sharp Williams, and Oscar W. Underwood. Chairmen of House committees—even of Appropriations or Ways and Means—would similarly leave the House to run for the Senate, or for governor.

In the context of the past 20 or 30 years such behavior is unthinkable. Since the 1920s no Speaker, majority leader, or minority leader has left the House to seek any other elective office. And the departure of major committee chairmen is almost as rare. Since the LaFollette-Monroney Act of 1946 the only chairman, or ranking minority member, of a major House committee to run for the Senate was Kenneth Keating—in New York in 1958—and he did so only under intense pressure and heavy prodding from such Republican figures as President Dwight D. Eisenhower, Vice President Richard Nixon, and Attorney General Brownell. Even from the lesser committees of the House, the only two men making the switch to the Senate were Everett M. Dirksen, top Republican on the unimportant House D. C. Committee, and Clair Engle, who had been chairman of the House Interior Committee prior to his election to the Senate from California.

Even before the Civil War a major lifetime political career could be carved in the Senate. Thomas Hart Benton's 29.5 years (1821-1851, defeated in his bid for a sixth term) is only one extreme example. Despite shifting party lines, the six-year term and the possibilities for maneuver within the legislative election at the state level made a longterm career possible. Since the Senate had only one-third of its membership up for election every two years, it operated as a continuing body. Committee selections generally were made as vacancies occurred, and once made they were usually held for as long as a senator served. The deposings of Stephen A. Douglas by the Democrats in the 1850s and of Charles Sumner by the Republicans in the 1860s were highly exceptional. Like the four-minute mile, serving 30 years in the Senate seemed an impossible goal. But once the barrier was broken by John Sherman of Ohio in 1895 and then by Justin Morrill of Vermont in 1897, careers of that length became commonplace. Since 1900 at least 20 additional senators have reached or passed the 30-year mark, with the all-time record (so far) going to Arizona's Carl Hayden.

The situation in the nineteenth-century House could hardly have been more different. Every two years a member's committee assignment and even his continued service were at the mercy not only of the voters but also of the majority party and the Speaker. A member of the minority might be, and often was, removed from House membership by resort to the notorious "contested-election" process. So-called contests could be claimed in almost any district, whether Maine or Georgia, and the candidate of the majority party in the House declared the winner. Until 1907 only three of 382 "contests" were resolved in favor of the candidate of the minority party! Improvements in election administration and heightened public sensitivity to fraud have almost completely eliminated this threat to a member's career. And nineteenth-century party nominations, made in the confusion of the delegate convention, were subject to little regulation.

If a member was fortunate enough to be renamed by his party, reelected by the voters, and escape a partisan challenge to his right to his seat, he would return to a House where committee assignments and chairmanships were openly bartered for in the process of determining the party leadership (especially in the majority party, which elected the Speaker). The support of freshmen members was courted as avidly, or more, than that of the relatively few veteran members. Thus after the Democrats captured the House in 1890, there was a sharp four-way fight for the Speakership among Roger Mills of Texas, who had been Ways and Means chairman in the 1887-1888 Congress, Charles Crisp of Georgia, William Springer of Illinois, and Benton McMillin of Tennessee. A long-time Washington reporter summarizes the contest as follows:

> On the first ballot in the caucus only a few votes separated Mills and Crisp, the leaders, and it was regarded as certain that one of them would be named. Then the dickering began among the managers of the candidates for high committee places, and the Crisp men outgeneraled the Mills forces in that line of work. Judge Springer withdrew his name and voted for Crisp, and that settled it. Mr. Crisp was nominated, and Judge Springer secured the chairmanship of the Ways and Means Committee, and, as the floor leadership went with it as usual, he was satisfied with the outcome. The other Crisp managers got important committee assignments.

The fluidity of the process is indicated by the events of the next Congress, also Democratic-controlled. Crisp, who had been Speaker, was reelected but faced a contest for the leadership with his former supporter, William Springer. When the jockeying was over, William Holman of Indiana, the famed "watchdog of the Treasury" and chairman of the Appropriations Committee in the preceding Congress, was moved to the chairmanship of Indian Affairs; and Springer, chairman of Ways and Means in the preceding Congress, was demoted to chairman of Banking and Currency—the new chairman of Ways and Means was William Wilson of West Virginia. To round out the story, in 1894 Speaker Crisp managed to get himself elected to the Senate (thus following former Speaker Carlisle), while Wilson, Springer, and Holman (the key committee chairmen) were all defeated. And the new chairman of Appropriations, Joseph Sayers, left the House in 1899 to serve as governor of Texas.

Translated into the House of the early 1960s, this would mean a sequence of events something like this: Speaker Rayburn would give up the Speakership to become a freshman senator and would be succeeded by John McCormack. After the next election McCormack would be challenged for the leadership by Wilbur Mills, who would then be dumped from Ways and Means and made chairman of Banking and Currency. Clarence Cannon, the latter-day watchdog of the Treasury, would be switched to the chairmanship of Interior. If this sounds a bit unlikely, consider further that McCormack would then leave the House to become a freshman senator, and that Mills, Cannon, and the new Ways and Means chairman might all be defeated at the next election. Cannon's successor on Appropriations, George Mahon, would serve a couple more terms and then run for governor of Texas. That is what the script would call for if current House politics were conducted nineteenth-century style!

Such a system provides flexibility, of one sort or another, but virtually rules out making a systematic career of serving in the House. The contrast can be seen by a quick comparison of the careers of the Democratic House chairmen of the 10 leading substantive committees (Appropriations, Ways and Means, Judiciary, Military, Naval, Commerce, Foreign Affairs, and Agriculture, Rivers and Harbors, and Banking and Currency) when Grover Cleveland took office in 1893 with the chairmen of the same committees when Franklin D. Roosevelt took office in 1933. Of the chairmen in 1933 seven were eventually carried out of the House office building feet first, and three retired (after serving an average of 33.3 years in the House). None of the 10 ever ran for any other office, and none of the 10 was ever upset in his home district. By contrast, of the 10 Cleveland chairmen four were defeated in 1894 and one in 1896. Two were elected to the Senate and subsequently served as governors, while a third went directly from the House to the governor's mansion. The 10 Cleveland chairmen served an average of 7.4 terms (in several cases with interruptions in service) and only one served more than 10 terms (he served 11). The 1933 chairmen served an average of 16.2 terms (better than 32 years) apiece, and only two served less than 10 terms, while three served more than 20 terms (prior to 1900 no member of the House had ever served that long). Of the 1933 chairmen four outlasted FDR and served with President Truman, three with President Eisenhower, two with President Kennedy, and one (Carl Vinson of Georgia) served with President Johnson (who in 1937 had been a freshman member of the committee of which Vinson was then chairman).

Lest it be thought that the House in the 1890s was atypical, it should be emphasized that a similar pattern prevailed from the end of the Reconstruction. Thus, of the seven regularly elected Speakers serving from 1870 to 1894, one was elected in his third term of service, two in their fourth term, two in their fifth (one of these having just returned to the House after being out a term!), one in his sixth (Reed, who had sought the Speakership unsuccessfully in his third term), and one in his seventh term. Of these seven, one (Kerr) died within a year of his selection as Speaker. Of the remaining six exactly half (Blaine, Carlisle, and Crisp) left the House to go to the Senate. Keifer, who had defeated Reed for the Republican choice in 1881, was denied renomination to the House in 1884. Randall, who had the longest service of the seven, was upset in the Democratic caucus of 1883, and he served the next three Congresses as chairman of the Appropriations Committee. Reed, embittered that McKinley rather than he had been nominated by the GOP for president in 1896 and out of sympathy with the Spanish-American War, resigned from the House and joined a Wall Street law firm.

Since the Speakership was obtained by the appropriate parceling out of committee chairmanships and memberships, these also were subject to substantial shifts as well as to the high turnover. Thus, Henry L. Dawes was chairman of Appropriations (1869-1870), then chairman of Ways and Means (1871-1874), and then went to the Senate. William Morrison was chairman of Ways and Means in 1875-1876, but lost the position to Fernando Wood in 1877-1880, only to return for 1883-1886. James A. Garfield went from chairman of Banking and Currency in 1869-1870 to chairman of Appropriations in 1871-1874. Frank Hiscock, congressman from Syracuse, New York, became chairman of Appropriations in his third term (1881-1882), subsequently served as a minority member on Ways and Means, and then was elected to the Senate. William Holman, one of the few really long-term nineteenth-century members, specialized in appropriations during Randall's chairmanship. But instead of succeeding Randall on the committee, Holman was switched to Public Lands in the Fiftieth and Fifty-first Congresses, and in the latter, the Republicans named Sayers of Texas as top minority man on Appropriations. In the Fifty-second Congress Holman returned to Appropriations as chairman, but in the succeeding Congress he again lost the post (to Sayers) and had to be satisfied with Indian Affairs.

Although total experience in the House was of some importance, continuous service meant virtually nothing prior to the twentieth century. The misuse of "election contests" meant that removal did not necessarily constitute rebuke, and the lack of reliance on seniority meant that many members dropped out for a term or so, held other offices and then returned, or came back to pick up their House service virtually unimpaired afterward. The lack of importance of continuous service was most obvious in the pre-Civil War era. Thus, Henry Clay served two short tours in the Senate before he ran for the House in 1810. Speaker Clay then resigned from the House in 1814 but came back again for the next three Congresses (in which he was again Speaker). He then skipped a whole Congress but returned for the next two (in which he was again Speaker). He returned to the increasingly important Senate in 1831, resigned in 1842, but returned once more in 1849. To the extent that continuous service constitutes a congressional career, Clay had no less than seven separate and distinct congressional careers, which is only to say that continuous service had nothing to do with his two real careers in the House and Senate. Indeed, Clay (as chairman of a select committee) fashioned the epic Compromise of 1850 at a time when his continuous service in the Senate dated from March 4, 1849!

In the nineteenth-century House, continuous service was even less important and defeat for a term (or being ousted in a "contest") had little or no effect. Michael Kerr was defeated in 1872 (after serving four terms) but came back in 1874 to be elected Speaker (when he had *zero* continuous prior service)! Joe Cannon was defeated in the Democratic sweep of 1890, but returned to Congress in 1892, and after the 1894 Republican victory, became chairman of the Appropriations Committee (he then had 10 terms of service but only one term of continuous prior service). Continuous prior service, then, was of no consequence for either standing on committee or election to party leadership. To understand how and why this was changed is to understand the twentieth-century Congress.

The extreme fluidity or even near chaos of the House in the 20-year span from 1875 to 1894 came to a sudden stop and was succeeded by a 16-year period (1895-1910) in which change in the House was virtually imperceptible. There was no change of party control in the latter period, and the "team" of leaders that Tom Reed brought to the top in 1893 continued to dominate the picture, with only a few replacements, up to 1910. Reed, who had done so much to mold the rules of the modern House, was also the master architect of the only real centralized "machine" to ever dominate that body over a substantial period of time. And it was the reaction in 1910 and 1911 against this centralized control that brought into being the "modern" House and further shaped the pattern of the House career.

Thus, there have been three main patterns of House politics, each with its particular type of career. Just as nature abhors a vacuum, so most politicians abhor excessive conflict and uncertainty. But conflict and uncertainty prevailed in the House up to 1895, and the stable oligarchy of 1895-1910 was destroyed by the events of 1910-1911. The great transformations in the structure of the House, and thus of House careers, were not the conscious result of any one man's will or of any one event. Rather they were the net result—often unintended—of a number of trends and decisions. As Marx once noted:

Men make their own history but they do not make it just as they please; they do not make it under circumstances as chosen by themselves but under circumstances directly found, given and transmitted from the past.

In retrospect it is not difficult to specify the crucial preconditions that served to maintain the fluidity of the nineteenth-century House. As these factors were changed, the career possibilities and motivations of the members were changed, and this amounted to a change in the political structure of the House. Table 1 lists more important preconditions for fluidity and the factors that changed. The cumulated effect of these changes was to make possible a new-style organization of the House under Speaker Cannon, but it proved intolerable. When Cannon was cut down to size, and the Democrats captured the Speakership, the "modern" House was the result. To go back to the centralized control of a Cannon, or the fluidity of the pre-1895 era would require changes in the crucial factors that underlie the origins of the modern House career pattern. Empty talk about changing the rules or practice of the House ignores this simple reality.

Table 1. *Factors Sustaining Fluidity and the Origins of Seniority in the House*

Nineteenth-Century Conditions	Changes in Conditions
1. Prior to the Civil War a member might be left off the roster by the clerk of the House in a move to effect majority control.	1. A member's right to a seat was not threatened in this way after the Civil War.
2. A member of the minority was always in danger of being unseated by a questionable "election contest," decided on strict partisan vote.	2. Improved election administration, and publicly supplied ballots made this unlikely after 1900.
3. Voluntary turnover was very high; the norm in some districts required rotation or a two-term limit (even Lincoln had been limited to a single term).	3. Efforts at reelection increased around the turn of the century; norms against reelection declined
4. Until the 1890s competition was on a much more even basis throughout the country than after 1900.	4. The 1896 campaign polarized the country, and local one-party dominance was reinforced by: a. Rise of white supremacy and decline of GOP in the South b. Urban-rural split c. Catholic-Protestant split d. Immigrant-native split
5. Party control of the House alternated frequently.	5. There was no alternation in party control of House from 1895 to 1911, and there has been only infrequent alternation since.

Table 1. *continued.*

---

6. All committees assignments, majority and minority, and all chairmanships were designated by the Speaker for each new Congress.

6. After 1902 the Speaker dealt with only his party's assignment, leaving minority assignments to the minority leader.

7. There was frequent competition for party leadership and rapid turnover of leaders (who frequently ran for the Senate).

7. Leaders became more likely to remain in the House, less likely to run for the Senate, and more difficult to challenge because of:
   a. Infrequency of alternation in power.
   b. Fact that the minority leader after 1902 was buttressed by power to make minority-committee assignments.

8. Few members had much seniority so there was no effective guide to apportioning positions.

8. After 1985 seniority and continuous service became more common and harder to ignore.

9. The House was not a continuing body, in law, in practice, or in most of its membership.

9. Although still not a continuing body in a legal sense, the House *has* become one in much of its practice and in the great majority of its membership.

In summary, the nineteenth-century pattern of flexibility reflected both the lack of continuity in membership (resulting from high turnover plus contested elections) and the lack of continuity of structure within the House (resulting from frequent alternation of party and movement of party leaders to the Senate). A change in the latter factor permitted a unique centralization of power under Reed and Cannon, but the situation was not as stable as it looked. The Democrats had never accepted the idea of a presiding "czar" (indeed, they had even opposed the Reed rules). And the spectacular drop in turnover produced inevitable pressures, even under Cannon, for adherence to seniority.

If not the best of all possible rules, seniority at least has the advantages of being an operational criterion and an automatic one, which "merit" or "ability" are not to an equal degree. It thus tended to avoid controversy and was soon wrapped in a glow of legitimacy. Length of continuous service on a committee soon became a legislative fetish, complete with special procedures for breaking ties. But it should be emphasized that new appointments to a committee continue to constitute a vital exception to the general reliance on seniority, especially in the House. No amount of seniority will guarantee a member admission to the elite committees, such as Rules, Ways and Means, or Appropriations. In the Senate, however, seniority is much more important as a criterion for making committee shifts; for the Republicans it is usually decisive.

Seniority is not a "rule" to be adopted or repealed, but a habit, a way of life, and a means of resolving conflict. It is used by the Supreme Court to determine its seating (and the assignment of opinions if the chief justice is not with the majority), by the District of Columbia's government in assigning license plates to diplomats, by unions to determine job rights, and by people throughout the world who line up in queues (whether at the A & P or Lenin's tomb). It rests on no very rational basis, but neither does monarchy or counting ballots. Since the basic reliance on seniority in Congress is unlikely to be reversed, it is all the more important that its sway be limited. This can be done by providing more democratic procedures within committees, by maintaining flexibility in the Committee on Committees where the Democratic reliance on Ways and Means to make committee appointment has the advantage of adding five new committee members when the party shifts from minority to majority position (thus bringing new blood into that crucial body), and by awareness that congressional careers can be—and in the past have been—organized on other bases.

THE SENATORIAL CAREER

The Senate career seems not to have changed much over the past hundred years, although the formal process of election and the types of individuals elected have been sharply altered. In contrast to the House, however, service in the Senate has from early in the nineteenth century constituted a potential lifetime career, in which seniority plays an important role. Recent descriptions of the Senate have made much of the true Senate type, the "inner club," the emphasis upon protecting each senator's rights, the lack of importance of speechmaking per se, and the importance of specialization. Walter Wellman, a perceptive Washington correspondent, hit on all these themes in a piece published in 1906, in which he described the great influence of Wisconsin Senator John C. Spooner:

> The Country's estimate of a public man does not always agree with the Washington estimate. When they conflict, Washington is usually much nearer the mark. . . . It is coldly critical; it studies at close range; it is behind the scenes. . . .
>
> The man who rises to the first rank in a body like the Senate is a man of power. Only ten or a dozen of fourscore and a half form that select company. . . . Accident or wealth may get a man into the Senate, but it will not get him into the inner circle. . . . The Senate is largely controlled by this inner circle of a dozen men. Actual personal leadership it will not have. According to the ethics and tradition of that body, no man may aspire to such commanding influence in it as Speakers have wielded or chairmen of Ways and Means Committees have enjoyed in the House. . . . It is a stickler for a theory of equality. . . . But in practice there is the dominating inner circle; and when one thinks of that circle, the first man who comes to mind is Spooner of Wisconsin.
>
> Influence in the Senate is acquired in many ways. The popular impression appears to be that it is best won by making speeches. . . . Some of the most influential men in the Senate do not speak at all, or but rarely. Some of the best and most prolific talkers have little influence. . . . A large measure of his [Spooner's] success is due to the fact that he rarely uses his energy or capitalizes his influence in the pursuit of trifles.
>
> In Congress, as everywhere, the tendency is toward specialization. Senators take up one line or another, become as proficient as possible in that, and give very little attention to other subjects. . . . He is so willing to work, so eager to investigate, so tireless and so alert, and his sincerity and judgment are so highly valued, that all the specialists consult him. . . . As a lawyer and maker of laws, as a watchdog against the furtive slipping in of blunders, as a suggester of stronger and better methods, as a deviser of practical schemes which will meet existing conditions in the Senate and the country, he is without a peer in public life. The natural result—despite himself, and not at all through his seeking—is that his

finger is felt in nearly every big legislative pie. His impress is more or less upon every policy, every great act.

It follows, as a matter of course, that such a man is much sought; that other senators are constantly running to him with their knotty problems; that to him come many opportunities to give his country the benefit of his talents.

The above analysis has hardly been improved upon by more recent students of the Senate. Still, change has taken place. The mind boggles at a Pierre Salinger moving to Rhode Island to challenge Nelson Aldrich in the 1900s. And there is no denying that business domination, by fair means and foul, of many nineteenth-century state legislatures, did lead to a period when many Senate seats (especially in the Northeast) came perilously close to being for sale. Shortly after the turn of the century one observer (not a muckraker) summarized the situation as follows: ·

> If you will take Montana's Clark, Senator Gorman, and Tom Patterson from the Democratic side of the Chamber, nearly all the wealth of the Senate will be on the Republican or rich East Side. There are ten Republican senators that represent one hundred million dollars, and ten others who are millionaires. There are only four or five millionaires on the Democratic side; as we rate wealth these days, twenty-five out of the thirty-one Democratic senators are comparatively poor men. . . . It is refreshing in these days of graft, however, to mention that it is an exceedingly rare case, where a senator from a Southern state is accused of fraud and bribery in gaining his seat in the Senate. . . .
>
> Take, for instance, John T. Morgan of Alabama, who is serving his fifth term in the Senate. He is a poor man, and yet consider what a great railroad president he would have made, and the vast fortune he would have acquired, had he entered the business world, instead of the political field. His long head is filled to the brim with brains. . . .

The extent to which the Senate had become a rich man's club by the turn of the century might have led to a constitutional crisis such as involved the British House of Lords in 1911 or the U.S. Supreme Court in 1937. As it happened, however, the trend toward corporate domination that developed in the Gilded Age was halted and then reversed by the informal undermining of the process of having senators chosen by state legislatures. As William Riker has shown, the practice of sending written legislative "instructions" on specific bills, or of forcing resignation of a state's senator had virtually disappeared by 1850. Throughout the latter half of the nineteenth century new and more democratic devices were developed to provide a clear, and sometimes legally binding, mandate for a candidate whom the legislature would elect pro forma.

Thus, everyone has heard of the debates between Lincoln and Senator Stephen A. Douglas, but few realize just why the two candidates were campaigning all over Illinois when the actual election would take place in the legislature. The answer is that direct popular campaigning by such celebrities was used to elect slates to the legislature, less as local representatives than as virtual members of an electoral college. Later, actual popularity poll elections were authorized, and Oregon made the results of its senatorial poll binding on the legislature. Thus the legislative arena, in which business control bulked so large, was outflanked, and long before the adoption of the Seventeenth Amendment. When direct election of senators finally became part of the Constitution (1913), it was *already* the existing practice in 29 or 30 of the states.

The direct election of senators and the spread of the direct primary for making nominations both tended to reduce the political life chances of the wealthy businessman or the skilled legislative bargainer. The gainers were those candidates skilled at making an impact on the public, whether on reform issues (as with LaFollette, Borah, Norris) or—in the South—the race issue (Vardeman, Tom Watson, and Bilbo). A well-known political name, such as Taft in Ohio, Talmadge in Georgia, Long in Louisiana, or Kennedy in Massachusetts, is a major political asset. And the real public figure—or celebrity—who has won fame in another field may well be able to cash it in for votes in a campaign for the senatorship: Consider only the enthusiasm generated for Astronaut John Glenn in Ohio, for football coach Bud Wilkinson in Oklahoma, or for Robert Kennedy in New York state, or the California Senate contest between White House press secretary Salinger and Hollywood's George Murphy. Once in office, the celebrity stands or falls on his political performance, but being a public "name" can be a great help in winning a nomination or election—especially in situations where party leaders evaluate the prospects as discouraging, or at best touch and go (the pro's willingness to fight for a nomination rests on a close estimate of the likelihood of winning). It is then that a party is most likely to look outside its own ranks for a candidate.

The steadily growing size of constituencies, both state and district (the average population of the latter has doubled since 1900), also makes the possession of at least some wealth a very substantial advantage. Tom Watson and Bob LaFollette could, in part, finance their political operations from the incomes received on the lecture circuit or from their own political magazines. Latter-day candidates find that they often must dip into their own income to acquire public exposure.

In modern times it is highly exceptional for a senator to leave that body for any other office. In earlier decades the Cabinet might have been tempting, but that is no longer the case. Of the state governorships only those in New York and California are likely to tempt a man away from the Senate, and then only if he has presidential ambitions. The presidency remains the great goal of American politics, a goal that has tempted even Speaker Rayburn and Senate leaders like Kerr, Russell, and Johnson. Just as leadership in the House is likely to take one out of the running for the Senate, so leadership in the Senate generally takes one out of the running for the presidency. Senate floor leaders, however, are frequently called upon as vice-presidential nominees—since World War I Republican floor leaders Curtis and McNary and Democrats Truman, Barkley, Johnson, and Humphrey were nominated as vice-presidents.

By contrast the House serves as a stepping stone for a wide range of offices. The decision to leave the House and try for the Senate is an especially tough one, since it involves giving up that post in order to seek a Senate nomination (except in the case of off-year elections to fill a Senate vacancy). But the members of almost any annual class of the House will be found to provide a number of future senators and governors. Thus the House class of 1946 included a larger-than-average group of 90 new members—by 1960 nine of the group had been elected to the Senate, and four others had left the House to wage unsuccessful campaigns. Among the better known House alumni of the class of 1946 were John F. Kennedy, Richard Nixon, George Smathers, Kenneth Keating, Jacob Javits, and Thruston Morton. The class of 1946 also has provided three governors, a federal district judge, and a number of administrators.

Chapter 3

Congress and the Evolution of
Legislative Professionalism

This chapter seeks to explore a variety of approaches to such long-run changes in legislative bodies as the "professionalization" of careers and emergence of strict committee seniority systems. The data are drawn largely from records of the U.S. House and Senate, but some of the processes may well be relevant for state legislatures. The material lends itself to a wide variety of analytic techniques, including transition probabilities, the Mover-Stayer Markov model,[1] cohort analysis, evolutionary patterns of development, causal modeling, or even computer simulation. Since the total available data are so vast, this is simply an exploratory study.

The chapter is organized into four main sections. The first section sets out various aspects of the general process of legislative "professionalization," and the second presents selected data relating to professionalization in the U.S. Senate and House. The third section examines the relevance of

---

This is a somewhat abbreviated version of the author's 1970 APSA paper on "Computer Simulation and Legislative 'Professionalism'," which appears in *Congress in Change*, ed. Norman J. Ornstein (New York: Praeger, 1975).

[1]Most of the discussion of this model has been omitted from this version of the paper.

membership stability for the emergence of strict committee seniority systems in the Senate (last quarter of 19th century) and then the House (first quarter of 20th century). The last section presents some concluding comments, along with a comparative view of contemporary state legislatures.

A GENERAL MODEL FOR
LEGISLATIVE "PROFESSIONALIZATION"

The current tendency to view the national Congress as marked by professionalism and low turnover whereas state legislatures are marked by part-time amateurs and high turnover is remarkably lacking in time perspective. In the beginning, all American legislative bodies were quite nonprofessional. Very high turnover and frequent resignations were hallmarks of the national Senate and House of Representatives throughout the entire pre-Civil War period. The Senate emerged as a highly stable professional body only after the end of Reconstruction. The House remained fluid, both in membership and in committee structure, up to the massive realignment of 1896. We are interested in the causes and consequences of the radical change that occurred.[2]

In general, any legislature will have some mixture of career types, but one type may be numerically predominant. By taking as our criteria a long-run career perspective and a close to full-time career involvement, one perceives the following four individual types of legislators:

"Amateur": Part-time and short-run perspective

"Professional": Full-time and long-run perspective

"Notable": Part-time but long-run (often of high status)

"Marginal": Full-time but short-run (often of low status)

---

[2] The best account of the 1896 realignment is E. E. Schattschneider, "United States: The Functional Approach to Party Government," in *Modern Political Parties*, ed. Sigmund Neumann (Chicago: University of Chicago Press, 1956). The effects on Congress were first pointed out by myself in my 1964 working paper for the American Assembly on "The Congressional Career," reprinted in *Congressional Behavior,* ed. Nelson W. Polsby (New York: Random House, 1971), 14-27. See also the comments of Walter Dean Burnham in his *Critical Elections and the Mainsprings of American Politics* (New York: W. W. Norton, 1971).

We are primarily interested in the shift from "amateur" to "professional," and in viewing the relative distribution of members within a legislative chamber as a macro-level characteristic of the legislature. This, in turn may have "structural effects" on individual members.

The "professional" legislature is different. In it disparity of influence among members is generally less. And the professional legislature achieves substantial capability to oversee and influence the bureaucracies of the executive branch in a way that the amateurs never can. But this capability is achieved at the cost of reduced openness to shifting sentiments in the electorate (the motto of the professional legislature might well be, "The incumbent is always right."). In the professional legislature, "representation" largely by the shifting stands of sophisticated members rather than by physical turnover of members from presumably homogeneous constituencies. The member of a professional legislature faces complex problems of organizational theory, not the simple dilemmas of Edmund Burke.

The classic study of the "amateur" legislative body is Oliver Garceau and Corrine Silverman's account of the Vermont legislature.[3] Such legislative bodies are open to very substantial concentration of power by presiding officers and great disparity of influence. They also have little capability to deal with a sophisticated bureaucracy. But then, such bodies are most typical of the smaller, less industrial, less urban, and less bureaucratized states.

The professional legislator, though, has long-run career goals, and these are subject to the risks of the electoral process. But a member's career goals may also be subject to very substantial risks, at least to his influence, due to internal chamber (or leadership) practices. And in the long-run, the members have a way of affecting chamber practices and leadership.

Such a system may operate to produce a rather stable proportion of new members and stable distributions of prior service. In the twentieth century, however, both the Senate and House have shifted rather substantially in the direction of much more prior service. In the nineteenth century, sharp reductions in the proportion of new members were associated with major changes in the electoral module—thus the rate went up with the age of Jackson and came sharply down after the realignment of 1896. Deliberate

---

[3]Oliver Garceau and Corrine Silverman, "A Pressure Group and the Pressured," *American Political Science Review* 48 (1954): 672-91.

efforts at intervention are difficult. Among sophisticated students of Congress, there is discussion of the need for compulsory retirement of congressmen or a limit on the number of terms or years served. This would dampen the system, but lack of congressional support for such changes may dampen the enthusiasm of advocates instead.

PROFESSIONALIZATION OF CAREERS: SENATE AND HOUSE

The so-called Clay Congresses (1811-25) mustered at no time more than twenty members who had served five terms each, while from 1789 to 1860 only forty exceeded six terms.

DeAlva S. Alexander[4]

We know that for the modern "professionalized" Senate and House, resignations from office are extremely rare, efforts at reelection are the norm, and successful reelection is overwhelmingly the case for the House and quite frequent for the Senate. But how frequent or infrequent were these during the formative period of this nation, and when did their rate of frequency begin to approach modern levels? We shall begin with the Senate.

The distinguished senators of the 1st Congress set the early career pattern for that chamber: They fled the Capitol—not yet located in Washington—almost as fast as was humanly possible. Five of the original 26 hastened to resign even before completing their initial terms, most of which were for only two or four years (they had drawn lots to determine who would serve two-, four-, or six-year terms). One chanced to die in office, and two who had been selected for short terms had the unusual misfortune to seek reelection and fail. Eight were reelected, but six of these had been on short terms. The remaining 10 managed to serve out their term (or sentence to obscurity), but did not seek another round. By the time the Capitol was moved from Philadelphia to the swamps of Washington, only two of the original 26 senators remained, and in two more years they were gone.

---

[4]*History and Procedure of the House of Representatives* (Boston: Houghton Mifflin, 1916), 306.

Career data on the early Senate is a morass of resignations, short-term appointees, elective replacements, and more resignations. There are no notable careers in terms of service. Rather, records are set by the same senator resigning the same seat in the same term twice (by coming back to it for a time after his initial replacement resigned), or by a single man's serving as a state's replacement for each of the state's two senate seats and quitting from each. From 1789 to 1801 the amazing total of 94 individuals (or 95, if one counts Albert Gallatin, who was admitted but then held ineligible) had warmed senatorial seats for varying times.

Among the most distinguished of the initial senators was Charles Carroll of Carrollton. He was a Maryland notable, a signer of the Declaration of Independence, and a delegate to the Continental Congress. He was reelected in 1792, but resigned later that year since he preferred being a state senator, in which position he served from 1777-1800 (Maryland had passed a law preventing individuals from serving in both state and federal legislatures concurrently). Carroll lived to almost the end of Jackson's first administration, but had left the Senate at the end of Washington's first administration.

In its initial decades, of course, the Senate was an honorific nothing. Everyone was for a second chamber in theory, but no one could figure out what—if anything—it should do in actual practice. Some states used their senatorships as a sinecure for defeated House members, and ambitious young politicians—Madison or Clay—were unanimous in vowing that they intended to avoid being stuck in that "do-nothing" chamber. How and why this came to change is itself an exciting story, but it cannot be pursued here. That it was a long time before it did change, however, is obvious from the careers of successive Senate cohorts.

Senate "cohorts" are a bit more awkward to define than are House "cohorts." There is the problem of the three classes of seats, with one-third coming up for election every two years. And there is the much greater role played by appointive or elective replacements. Many of the appointive replacements did not seek or expect election, and including them with the more regular senators tends to confuse the picture a bit. For exploratory purposes we have adopted the simple, though hardly ideal, expedient of taking as "cohorts" all those senators who were on hand at the beginning of a given Congress. We have then pursued their careers through to the end of their current terms, about one-third coming up for election every two years. This should not effect the probability of their seeking reelection or not, but it does somewhat reduce (to an average of about four years) the time in which they might resign from office. The advantage is that most of the very temporary interim appointees are thus eliminated, and we can concentrate on more or less "regular" senators. This also means that looking at such a "cohort" for a given Congress gives us data not just on the one-third elected to that Congress, but also on those (or their replacements) who were elected to the previous two Congresses. Conversely, data on Congresses less than six years apart include some overlap.

Up to about 1840 those who sought and won an additional term did not differ much from the original cohort. Thus of the eight senators reelected from the original 26, no less than four (including Charles Carroll of Carrollton) resigned in the course of their new term. From the cohort of the 9th Congress (1805) 14 are reelected, but five of these resign. From the 11th Congress six are reelected, but four of these resign. From the 24th Congress (1835) 16 are reelected, but nine resign. The Civil War intrudes to preclude this analysis for the 1850s, but a marked shift is evident in the 1840s. The cohorts of 1841, 1845, and 1849 show, with some overlap, a total of 35 members reelected, but only three of these resign in their subsequent term. Here we have a glimmer of hope for the emergence of "stayers." Indeed, in the 1850s the dominant southern Democrats dig in their heels and hang on for all they are worth. As a result even average terms of service shows a modest gain.[5]

Prior to the Civil War one just did not make a long-run "career" out of continuous Senate service, except perhaps as a fluke. Since no positions in the Senate rested on any form of seniority (in the chamber or on committees) major political figures drifted in and out of the Senate as convenience dictated. Cabinet posts were a major attraction, luring both Clay and Webster for a time. The less well known John J. Crittenden served four separate tours in the Senate off and on from 1817 to 1861, interspersing these with two stretches in the Cabinet (attorney-general), a tour as governor of his state, an appointment to the Supreme Court (for which his former colleagues refused confirmation), and some other posts; at his death he was a member of the House of Representatives. Lateral movement from Senate to Cabinet and then *back* to the Senate was particularly important in

---

[5]See Figure II in Randall B. Ripley, *Power in the Senate* (New York: St. Martin's Press, 1969), 46.

the nineteenth century, but was a practice that could not easily be combined with a strict committee seniority system.

In the twentieth century one can pick almost any year and then turn to the Senate of a decade earlier and find at least one-fourth, sometimes one-third, and recently around one-half of the same individual members serving in a continuous stretch. Put another way, the political "half life" of a Senate cohort over the past decade has been close to 10 years. But for the pre-Civil War Senate, it is rare to find more than two or three stray senators who might be on hand at points 10 years apart. Thus Table 1 contrasts the number of such 10-year veterans for selected Congresses in both the nineteenth and twentieth centuries:

The long-term survivors in the earlier periods do include such historically important figures as Webster (from the 21st to 26th Congress), Clay and Calhoun (both from the 26th to the 31st), and Stephen A. Douglas (31st to 36th). But three of these four served "broken" Senate careers, the longer portion of which managed to span a five-Congress period.

After the Civil War and Reconstruction, the Senate was at a peak of influence. The executive branch was in a long eclipse, and senators extended their sway into effective control of state party machines (or vice versa). The national government was by then of vital importance in regard to tariff policy, monetary policy, and—for the South—race policy. Senators controlled the allocation of federal patronage, and increasingly lorded it over the House. Thus by the 49th Congress (1885) resignations were only one-third the number for 1845, though the Senate was 20 members larger. The ratio of members seeking reelection to those not doing so is no longer half and half, but stands at 55 to 13. By this time most states were predominantly either Democratic or Republican so that electoral hazards were reduced. By this time also, Senate committee chairmanships were being quite rigorously handled in terms of continuous committee service. The Senate was a good place for a politician to be. And the longer he stayed there the better it would be. By the end of the century Thomas Hart Benton's record of 30 years service was beaten, and the Senate hailed its first six-term veteran.

But let us turn to the House of Representatives. It got off to a somewhat more impressive start than the Senate but did not really shift into modern gear until the generation following the 1896 realignment. In an excellent senior honors thesis Richard Morningstar collected data on the careers of

Table 1. *Senate Veterans Serving over Ten Years for Particular Congresses Indicated*

Period of Service	Number Serving	From Total in Base Year	
1st to 6th Congress:	3	26	
6th to 11th Congress:	2	32	
11th to 16th Congress:	3	34	
16th to 21st Congress	9	44	
21st to 26th Congress:	4	48	
26th to 31st Congress:	8	52	
52d to 57th Congress:	22	88	
62d to 67th Congress:	29	96	
72d to 77th Congress:	28	95	(plus a vacancy)
82d to 87th Congress:	42	96	
86th to 91st Congress:	52	100	

all members who left the House in three different periods.[6] The crucial importance of distinguishing between alternative reasons for turnover is evident in Morningstar's comparisons between the periods 1811-20 and 1887-96. Both are marked by very high turnover. But for the earlier period only 49 of 465 departures could be attributed to electoral defeat; for the latter period electoral defeat accounted for 309 of 750. What the early House lacked was not safe seats, but a desire and incentive to retain one's seat. In the late nineteenth century the desire for reelection was up somewhat, but reelection had become much more risky.

In 1964 I argued that changes in the structure of the House career were crucially linked to the massive political realignment of the 1890s.[7] This

---

[6]Richard Morningstar, "Congress as a Closed System: Its Characteristics and Implications" (senior honors thesis, Harvard, 1967). The author analyzes House careers for the three periods 1811-20, 1887-96, and 1951-60.

[7]See H. Douglas Price, "Congressional Career."

decade was marked by the emergence of the really solid Democratic South, by the rapid spread of ballot reform and registration systems, but above all by the collapse of the Democrats in the 1896 Bryan campaign. Democratic gains in the silver states and some farming states proved temporary, but massive Democratic losses in the Northeast and Midwest were to last until Al Smith and the Great Depression. As a result, reelection became more probable, and more incumbents came to seek reelection. Successive new all-time records for amount of prior service in the House were set in 1900, then a higher record in 1904, then a yet higher record in 1906, and that one was broken in 1908. Successive new all-time low records for proportion of new members were set in 1898, again in 1900, again in 1904, and yet again in 1908.

Table 2 presents the career dispositions of five House cohorts. These include a Federalist Congress (2d), a Democratic-Republican Congress (12th), a Jacksonian Congress (24th), a post-Reconstruction Congress (49th), and a post-1896 Republican Congress (59th). The crucial point of what might be termed the Schattschneider-Price theory is that the realignment of 1896 sharply reduced the number of competitive House districts, leading to a steady increase in the number of committed "stayers" in the House. Thus the 1885 cohort of 325 House members produced only 193 who were reelected to the following Congress; the slightly larger 1905 cohort produced 279 members reelected to the following Congress. Of the 1885 group, 70 had not even sought reelection and 49 who did were defeated. Of the 1905 group only 44 did not seek reelection and only 42 were defeated.

There are at least three alternative theories that have been suggested more or less in lieu of the Schattschneider-Price emphasis on realignment leading to careerism. Nelson W. Polsby has sought to describe change in the House in terms of "institutionalization." There is some very useful literature relating to this process in various contexts, but the term is more useful for description than for historical explanation (it could, of course, be taken in the factor analysis sense of a single unobservable factor that underlies change in the observed variables).

A second alternative, frequently suggested, is of relatively steady incremental change in House careers. If this were the case then one might expect to pick up at least some trace of it from a simple linear regression over time. We ran this for both percentage of freshman members and for average terms prior service, using Stuart Rice's data, for all pre-1900 Con-

Table 2. *House Careers from Pre-1800 to Post-1896: Performance in Office of Five House Cohorts Consisting of Members on Hand at Opening of Congresses Indicated*

	Number of Cases from House Cohort Indicated				
Congress:	2nd	12th	24th	49th	59th
Year:	1791	1811	1835	1885	1905
Entering Cohort	68	143	242	325	386
Serve Out Term	65	136	224	311	365
Resign in Term	2	5	13	5	8
Die during Term	0	1	5	8	12
Unseated	1	1	0	1	1
Seek Reelection	43	92	137	242	321
Do not run for Reelection	22	44	87	70	44
Reelected	43	80*	114	193*	279*
Defeated	0	12	23	49	42

*Includes one or more who resigned after reelection but before opening of next Congress.

gresses except for the very 1st Congress (i.e., for the 2nd through 56th). The results show no relationship whatsoever; the pre-1900 experience is not one of simple trend (though for the period after 1900, of course, there is a substantial trend).

A third alternative view is that the seeming change from nineteenth- to twentieth-century patterns is, in large measure, spurious. It simply rests on the admission of new states and creation of new seats. This raises a useful point; the new members due to creation of new seats should indeed be considered. But doing this does not begin to account for the massive difference between nineteenth- and twentieth-century figures. With the exception of Oklahoma, no new state has begun its representation in the House with more than two members, and most received one. Seats were transferred between states in the nineteenth century—just as they still are in the twentieth century—but this only affects every fifth Congress. Following the 1970 census 11 new seats were created for the 1972 elections (including five in California and three in Florida), but turnover in 1972 was less than one-half of what one finds for nineteenth-century elections in which absolutely no new seats were involved.

As it happens, the House made a strenuous effort to hold the line on size from the 1843 figure (which was actually reduced from the previous decade) down to the 1870 census (at which time substantial expansion began again). This was the era of greatest turnover for the House, but at most elections there were no new seats at all and only for the postcensus elections (for every fifth Congress) were the number of new seats of any real consequence.

Of the noncensus related elections, only 1844 involved more than one or two new seats, and it included only four (for Texas, Florida, and Iowa). Thus the elections of 1854 through 1860 included no new seats, but two of these generated over 50 percent freshmen and the other two more than 45 percent freshmen. By contrast, the 1958 election was a partisan "landslide" and included new seats for Hawaii and Alaska, but generated well under 20 percent freshmen.

The "new seats" hypothesis does explain the more or less regular "peaks" in which nineteenth-century turnover is up some 10 percent, say from 40 to 50, but it does not begin to explain why the ordinary level in the absence of any new seats is at 40 percent rather than the modern level of around 15 percent. That shift, and not the mild peaking in the nineteenth century, is the big problem and "new seats" is simply not the main explanation. It is, however, a complication that needs to be considered in dealing with the data on turnover. For the Senate, incidentally, where the more-or-less uninhabited new states get two senators each right from the start, creation of new seats is more of a consideration.

Somewhat related to the "new seats" theory is the problem that overall national levels of turnover and careerism tend to conceal very marked state and sectional differences. The case for disaggregation by Fiorina, Rohde, and Wissel, is very strong and extremely interesting.[8]

---

[8]Norman J. Ornstein, *Congress in Change: Evolution and Reform* (New York: Praeger, 1975).

FROM COMMITTEE STABILITY TO
COMMITTEE SENIORITY: A COMPARATIVE VIEW

My long service here and the custom which has obtained almost from the beginning of the Government entitles me to select from among the committees of which I am a member a chairmanship. I am senior Democrat on three important committees and can select the chairmanship of either one of them: Appropriations, Interstate Commerce, and Naval Affairs.

Senator Benjamin R. Tillman
(in personal letter to Woodrow Wilson, January 21, 1913)[9]

Congressional memories are often shorter than congressional careers. "Pitchfork" Ben Tillman was neither a good historian nor, in this case, a good prophet. Assigning committee chairmanships by seniority of committee service was not at all a practice obtaining "almost from the beginning of the Government." It had been more or less consciously adopted by the Democrats in the Senate when they found themselves in the majority, for the first time since the Civil War, in 1879. It clearly had not been followed by the Republicans in the decade of the 1870s, though after 1881 both parties seem to have abided by it with very few, usually minor, exceptions. By the time Tillman came to the Senate in 1895, it was indeed the accepted norm. Seniority had not been visible in the Senate to Woodrow Wilson in 1885 (but then he did not bother to look). But it was accurately described in 1895 by Clara H. Kerr and appears in even greater detail in McConachie's excellent 1898 book on *Congressional Committees.*[10]

Historians, apparently borrowing from each other, usually cite Stephen A. Douglas in 1859 and Charles Sumner in 1871 as the great "exceptions" to the general rule of Senate seniority. In fact, neither seems at the time to have been debated in those terms at all. But in 1913 Senator Tillman, then entering his fourth consecutive term, did become a sensational exception.

---

[9]U.S. Congress, Senate, Senator Tillman, personal letter to Woodrow Wilson, 63d Congress, special session, March 17, 1913, *Congressional Record*, CI, vol. 50, p. 31.

[10]See Clara S. Kerr, *Origin and Development of U.S. Senate* (New York: Andrus & Church, 1895), and Lauros G. McConachie, *Congressional Committees* (New York: Crowell, 1898).

In his letter to President-elect Wilson, quoted above, Tillman had gone on to indicate that he would take whichever chairmanship Wilson thought would make him most useful to the administration. But Tillman's letter sounds most enthusiastic in discussing what he could do as chairman of the Appropriations Committee.

In fact, Tillman could probably have best served the Wilson administration by just dropping dead. He was an eccentric, one of the few senators to be officially censured by that body, and certainly not the type to try and guide a complex legislative program. Wilson, caught in the throes of a presidential transition, finally wrote back his thanks. Detecting Tillman's seeming preference for Appropriations, Wilson graciously endorsed the idea.

Six weeks later the Democratic caucus denied Tillman the chairmanship he desired, and the angry senator splashed his correspondence with Wilson in the *Congressional Record.* The Democrats did very little other violence to the seniority rule,[11] finding it easier to put new members on so as to "pack" committees, or even to create new committees (as with Banking and Currency). Wilson's problem was that the official Democratic "leader" (a post not yet jelled into its modern form) was Thomas S. Martin, a conservative Virginian and anti-Wilson spokesman. The solution to Wilson's problem was to replace Martin with the progressive workhorse from Indiana, John W. Kern. But this needed to be done gracefully, and that could most easily be accomplished by easing Martin—who was number four on the Appropriations Committee—into its busy chairmanship. Second- and third-ranking Democrats already held major chairmanship.

---

[11]Claude G. Bower's biography, *The Life of John Worth Kern* (Indianapolis: Hollenback Press, 1918), is helpful on many things, but distinctly superficial on the details of the 1913 Senate committee slating. Aside from the Tillman incident, Kern seems to have followed the modern tactic of accepting seniority but undermining its importance by means of committee "stacking" and emphasizing that a majority of committee members could take control away from the chairman. This latter step created some controversy at the time. But the pattern was often repeated in regard to chairmen opposed to Wilson's wartime policies. There remains an important substantive question of just when the Senate Republicans and Democrats adopted the practice of letting chamber seniority determine priority for intercommittee transfers (a norm ended for the Democrats by the "Johnson rule" of 1953, but only watered down by the Republicans in recent years).

Kern could replace Martin as leader, and Martin could be chairman, if only Tillman could be induced to take the chairmanship of Naval Affairs. But Wilson had thrown away the key to the situation by his letter of six weeks earlier. In a sense, however, Tillman had undermined his claim to Appropriations by offering to take any one of the three chairmanships. Armed with this knowledge the caucus voted the Appropriations post to Martin, Kern became floor leader (where he virtually created the modern role of majority leader), and Tillman was left with Naval Affairs.

For almost a century, violations of seniority in the Senate have been few and far between. What at first appears as a possible violation usually turns out to be a choice among chairmanships, a question of third-party status, or explained by a break in a senator's continuous service. The Senate seems almost fated to be the inventor of seniority: The chamber has a continuous existence, only one-third of the members come up for election every two years, and it lacks a powerful presiding officer who might dominate appointments or use them for bargaining (as in House speakership contests).

For the House there could be noquestion of modern-type "seniority" until membership turnover was reduced to a level such that there was substantial continuity of committee service. Such *de facto* stability tends to generate demands for *de jure* seniority. But members' demands for seniority, or even for general stability, can still be frustrated by any one of several mechanisms. Thus in the Senate, open balloting for committee positions precluded the emergence of much stability. For the House three obvious mechanisms worked against the establishment of seniority:

1. Internal scramble for leadership. So long as the Speaker made all appointments, both of members and committee chairmen, candidates within the majority party campaigned for the speakership nomination largely in terms of promises to make, or maintain, such appointments. This is still common in many state legislatures and was the dominant pattern for the U.S. House of Representatives from the Civil War to the realignment of 1896. It is, of course, strengthened by relatively frequent alternation of majority control, and by relatively frequent change of Speakers. This was the case for pre-1896, but not the case after 1896, when the Republicans had a commanding lead until 1910.

2. Executive interference. This was common in the pre-Civil War House, and was blatant under Jefferson and Jackson. Subservient Speakers ran the risk of having the power of committee appointment removed. The

House came within two votes of this in 1806, and in 1832 the Speaker had to break a tie vote to preserve his authority to appoint the select committee to investigate Nicholas Biddle and the National Bank (a subject of prime concern to Andrew Jackson).

3. Cohesive legislative majority. This has been the ideal of academic supporters of "responsible parties," but has only rarely developed in Congress. Thaddeus Stevens and the Radical Republicans are probably the best example of this, although the Democrats did rather well in 1911 and throughout most of Wilson's first term (during which the pattern became more one of executive interference via the legislative caucus).

Internal scrambles for leadership in which committee chairmanships are the pawns have not occurred since the 1890s; successful executive interference ended with Woodrow Wilson; party caucuses have done little to enforce cohesion since 1919. When the Republicans took over the House in that year they voted against former Speaker Cannon's protégé, James Mann, who had been minority leader, and for a mild-mannered nonentity. Just for insurance they also voted for Mann's proposal to lodge the power of recommending committee appointments to the House in a committee on committees.[12]

In the late nineteenth century House chairmanships were won or lost as a side product of the bargaining involved in the recurrent scrambles for the Speakership. Often the same men hung on, but the dynamics of the process were such that each and every position was always available and might well

---

[12]From 1889 to 1919 the parties differed sharply on the role of the Speaker. Had the Republicans nominated Mann for Speaker in 1919 and given him the power of committee appointment, the old "autocratic" style of operation would have had a new lease on life. It is ironic that the Cannon-Mann wing of the Republicans, having lost the Speakership nomination, made the final move to nail down the Democratic-style "syndication" of the Speakership even for the Republicans. Polsby et al., in "The Growth of the Seniority System," quote *The New York Times* account, which emphasizes that the Mann proposal (for a committee on committees, with a member from each state electing a Republican but casting a weighted vote equal to the number of Republicans from the member's state) was a victory for long-term members who desired to protect their seniority. Poor Speaker Gillette was from the medium-sized state of Massachusetts, which would cast only 12 votes. Mann's Illinois got 20 votes, a number exceeded only by New York and Pennsylvania.

be drawn into the bargaining game. This is clear in descriptions of the operation of every Speaker from the Civil War to the end of the century. Here we shall quote but two.

> Speaker Kerr in 1875: "He asked Marble [NYC Democratic editor and publisher] for help in the selection of chairmen for major committees and even 'peremptorily' insisted that Marble come to Washington to help draw up the slate. Kerr placed Randall [his rival for Speaker] at the head of Appropriations but was in a quandary as to Ways and Means since both Wood and Cox felt that their services to the party and to Kerr in the caucus merited the assignment. Eventually he made William H. Morrison of Illinois head of Ways and Means, Cox of Banking and Currency, and ignored Wood's claims to a position of honor."[13]

> Speaker Crisp in 1891: "On the first ballot in the caucus only a few votes separated Mills and Crisp, the leaders, and it was regarded as certain that one of them would be named. Then the dickering began among the managers of the candidates for high committee places, and the Crisp men outgeneraled the Mills' forces in that line of work. Judge Springer withdrew his name and voted for Crisp, and that settled it. Mr. Crisp was nominated, and Judge Springer secured the chairmanship of the Ways and Means Committee and, as the floor leadership went with it as usual, he was satisfied with the outcome. The other Crisp managers got important committee assignments."[14]

Alleged "seniority" simply had nothing to do with it. Some of the same chairmen might continue, but in principle every chairmanship was at stake every two years. As Polsby *et al.* show,[15] the percentage continuing or

---

[13]In Albert V. House, "The Speakership Contest of 1875: Democratic Response to Power," *Journal of American History* 52 (1965): 272.

[14]O. O. Stealey, *Twenty Years in the Press Gallery* (New York, privately published, 1906), 106. This fascinating collection, by a variety of experienced Washington reporters, includes chapters on 11 Congresses, 48th to 58th, plus biographical studies of over a score of leading House members. There is not a single reference to committee seniority, although there is a great deal of discussion of the making of committee slates.

[15]Nelson W. Polsby, Miriam Gallaher, and Barry Rundquist, "The Growth of the Seniority System in the U.S. House of Representatives," *American Political Science Review* 63 (1969): 787-807.

moving up tended to be high or low depending upon whether there was a change of parties and of party leaders, a change of leaders within same party, or simply an alternation of party.

This pattern continued so long as there was high membership turnover, rapid alternation of party control, and frequent change of party leaders (many preferring to trade the Speaker's post for a seat in the more stable Senate). But all three of these conditions were upset by the realignment of 1896. For 14 years the Republicans held the majority, more and more of the members sought a permanent career in the House, and soon "Czar" Joseph Cannon was embarked on his record tenure as Speaker.

Up to the turn of the century, House members quite literally did not understand what "seniority" was in the modern sense of continuous service on a party's list of committee members. Thus in 1895, after the Republicans recaptured the House, two leading Republican members (Nelson Dingley and Sereno Payne) *both* claimed the chairmanship of Ways and Means. Each claimed knowledge of the tariff and "seniority," though in fact Dingley was not even a member of the committee and had not been for the past four years. He had gone off the committee to make room for former Speaker Reed during the two Congresses the Republicans were in a minority (1891-95). Dingley, who had no continuous service on the committee, got the chairmanship.

Strict seniority, which had meant almost nothing in the House as of 1900, had come to mean almost everything in naming committee chairmen and ranking members by 1920. Michael Abram, in his excellent senior honors thesis on the subject, concludes that "after 1925 seniority stood as the sole criterion of committee advancement with only the insignificant exceptions we have noted,"[16] and sees the major shift as occurring between 1913 and 1919.

There are two broad classes of explanations for the emergence of seniority in the House between 1910 and 1920. The traditional one, more or less embraced by both Polsby et al. on the one hand and Joseph Cooper and Michael Abram on the other,[17] concentrates on the celebrated 1910

---

[16]Michael E. Abram, "The Rise of the Modern Seniority System in the U.S. House of Representatives" (Harvard honors thesis, 1966).

[17]Michael Abram and Joseph Cooper, "The Rise of Seniority in the House of Representatives." *Polity* 1 (1968): 52-85.

"revolt" against Speaker Cannon, and the reasons for the collision between the Republican "insurgents" and the Republican Speaker. The emphasis is on the tension and its causes. In my 1964 paper, I sought to minimize the importance attached to the strains of 1910, and instead argued that from 1896 on, career patterns and expectations had undergone basic structural change. Without this change a little conflict in the House, a common thing in any decade, would have meant little. Given the basic change, any old issue or conflict might serve to challenge the old order.

Moreover, the 1910 revolt did not touch the Speaker's power to make committee appointments. That more basic change was carried out by the Democrats in 1911. They had denounced the arbitrary power of the Speaker and promised changes in the 1908 Democratic platform. They had denounced Cannon for almost a decade, and had denounced Reed for most of the decade before that. Thus Cannon was operating on a very partisan Republican interpretation of the Speakership; any Democratic majority would be expected to alter the rules of the game. And Cannon himself was operating in a quite different House climate, where stability of membership and of committee service had assumed unparalleled proportions. As the years rolled by, there were no wide open Speakership contests that invited and necessitated widespread juggling of committee posts.

The extent of the stability that had settled on the House in the Republican era of 1895-1910 is impressive. If one had asked in 1910 who held the all-time record for longest service as chairmen of the 14 most important substantive committees of the House (DeAlva S. Alexander's list of 15, minus the Elections Committee) in 13 of the 14 cases the all-time record would have been set (or in two cases only tied) by chairmen of the 1895-1910 era. Members were, as a matter of plain observable fact, waiting in line for years. Increasingly, they wanted their waiting recognized, and their positions on the committee ladders protected. Around 1904 the *Congressional Directory* shifted from its former alphabetical listing with prior service indicated, to its modern-type listing in order of continuous service. Cannon did not shift his style, and the *Congressional Directory* goes on but Cannon was shunted aside.

The pressures for stability, continuity, and what amounted to seniority were hard to resist. This was something new for the House. Cannon's autocratic style reflected neither the fluidity of the nineteenth-century House nor an appropriate response to the stability of the modern House. "Cannonism" was an aberration that could not last. It was ended not by the insurgents, but by a new Democratic majority that was committed to change. There were still the three major mechanisms that might prevent the emergence of Senate-style seniority in the House. But bargaining for committees as part of the scramble for leadership was over, as the power to appoint committees was removed from the Speaker and lodged with a plural body (by the Democrats in 1911, and by the Republicans at the end of World War I). Executive interference existed for a time with Wilson and the Democratic caucus, but this pattern was disrupted by war issues and eventually led to disenchantments. After the war, one would not look for interference from the likes of Warren G. Harding. This left party cohesion, but the old party loyalty of post-Reconstruction days was fading, and was disrupted by new issues of progressivism and then war. McKinley had been a Civil War major, but Harding was born after Lee's surrender. For a time the Republicans put up a bold front against LaFollette and his outright party bolt, but by the mid-1920s the party found it easier to relax and embrace dissidents ranging from LaFollette, Jr., to the Non-Partisan League in North Dakota, Fiorello LaGuardia in Manhattan, and most of the agrarian radicals. Nothing was left to challenge the sway of seniority in the House or the Senate.

CONCLUSION

At the national level the triumph of legislative "professionalism" and of committee seniority are virtually complete. But the importance of seniority for its effect on policy outcomes has been diminishing. Within the Democratic party, the South now has far fewer safe seats or even states, and an increasing number of quite safe seats are to be found outside the South. Moreover, the question of who has seniority is becoming less important as more and more congressional committees adopt internal rules and reforms that make the chairmanship a role of very limited importance. Seniority, like monarchy, may be preserved by being deprived of most of its power. When chairmen merely reign, in the fashion of constitutional monarchs, then the question of just who should hold the position, and by what criteria, ceases to be a burning issue.

For anyone interested in the variety of historical patterns of organization presented by the House and Senate in the nineteenth century, the current range of state legislative practices have a quite familiar look. One does not need to go, like Darwin, to the Galapagos Islands to rediscover long missing species of legislative operation. The Alabama legislature, for example, is still typically as executive-dominated as was the national House in the days of Jefferson or Jackson. Belle Zeller noted in 1950 that all 14 Alabama House committees were headed by freshmen members.[18]

But state legislatures are changing. The New York legislature has long posted reelection rates that are quite comparable to the national House. Thus Charles Hyneman found for 1925-35 that the New York lower house averaged only 17.7 percent freshmen. Freshmen members in California have dropped from the 40.7 percent noted by Hyneman to the 17 percent reported by John Wahlke and Heinz Eulau. For New Jersey the comparable figures are 37.2 for 1925-35 and 15 percent for Wahlke-Eulau.[19]

One can make a direct comparison between turnover in the nineteenth-century House and the 1925-35 turnover rates found by Hyneman. A sustained effort is under way to "upgrade" state legislatures, largely by means of better pay, long (or unlimited) sessions, and other tangible benefits (staff, offices, etc.). A few years ago only three states had pay and allowances amounting to $10,000 per year; as of 1970 this is up to 11 states. For California—a leader in this trend—the biennial pay and allowances now come to $48,950 (a figure that compares well with the pay of most full professors).

In the 1960s the advance of professionalism at the state level has been slowed by recurring reapportionment crises. But when this settles down—beginning in 1972—many state chambers may find themselves in situations similar to the national House after 1896. The experience of both Senate and House suggests the strength of the drive for committee stability and then committee seniority once the membership of the chamber stabilizes. For the states, of course, there are the three counter-seniority mechanisms: internal scramble for leadership, outside executive and party interference, and the possibility of strong legislative cohesion.

---

[18]Belle Zeller, ed., *American State Legislatures* (New York: Thomas Y. Crowell, 1954).

[19]Charles S. Hyneman, "Tenure and Turnover of Legislative Personnel," *Annals of the American Academy of Political and Social Science* 195 (1938): 22-30. For the more recent figures for California and New Jersey see John Wahlke, Heinz Eulau et al., *The Legislative System* (New York: John Wiley & Sons, 1962).

How important for a legislative body is a sharp drop in membership turnover, or a switch from a single authority appointing committees to having this done by party committees? For a single given legislative body this is a difficult question indeed. But the American case affords us a rich body of varied experience both over time and by making comparisons between Senate and House and state legislatures. It is comparison between legislative bodies, focusing on different time periods, that can give us significant leverage on the tough questions. I hope future research will continue to move in these directions.

Chapter 4

House Turnover and the
Counterrevolution to Rotation in Office

ABSTRACT

The central theme of this work is the influence of an idea upon practical politics, specifically the principle of rotation in office, as it influenced the character and composition of the U.S. House of Representatives. After outlining the status of rotation during the nation's first half-century, the analysis turns to the impact upon the House of rotation norms after 1824, as seen in newly available data for preelection withdrawals and general election defeats.

The two main components in House turnover have trends that are related to a strong rotation impulse during the antebellum period and to the eclipse in rotation's popularity between the Civil War and the turn of the century. The data are inclusive for the years 1824-1976 and indicate that continuing declines in senior incumbent defeat rates from 1906-1960 derived in part from the growing preferences for expertise and professionalism.

The near monopoly of careerism in the modern House is seen not only as a radical departure from the past, but as the aftermath of a counterrevolution. For the ascendancy of the idea of professional congressmen first required a revolt, against a principle long prominent, that itself sprang from the American Revolution.

INTRODUCTION

The two centuries since the American Revolution have seen the eclipse in Congress of a longstanding principle of government. Under the Articles of Confederation maximum congressional service was three years in six; in order, argued Thomas Jefferson, "To prevent every danger which might arise to American freedom by continuing too long in office the members of the Continental Congress. . . ."[1]

After 1789 rotation in the legislative branch was no longer obligatory by law. In practice, however, turnover continued so sweeping that, as late as the nation's centennial year, members of the U.S. House of Representatives averaged less than one prior term in that chamber.[2]

During the 20th century the constitutional system of biennial elections has not prevented the House from rivaling in tenure both the U.S. Supreme Court and the Senate.[3] Average tenures in the three bodies since World War II are as follows: Supreme Court, 10.9 years; Senate, 10.4 years; House, 10.2 years.[4]

---

[1]Articles of Confederation, article V; Merill Jensen, *The Articles of Confederation* (Madison, Wisconsin: University of Wisconsin Press, 1940), 126, 130, 133-34; Thomas Jefferson, *The Papers of Thomas Jefferson*, ed. Julian F. Boyd, 17+ vols. (Princeton, N.J.: Princeton University Press, 1950-), 1:411.

[2]Stuart A. Rice, *Quantitative Methods in Politics* (New York: Alfred A. Knopf, 1928), 296-97, Table 46. From 1789-1876 the typical election gave upwards of half the House to newcomers. The election of 1882 was the last in history to put into the House more newcomers than incumbents. Incidentally, among the members of this final freshman majority was the author's great-granduncle, Rep. Isaac Struble of Iowa.

[3]Senators are defeated with about twice the frequency per election as congressmen. The 1914-76 average outside the South in percentage of incumbent candidates defeated in general elections, was 27 percent for the Senate and 12 percent for the House. Source: Appendix I, and for Senate figures, *Congressional Quarterly's Guide to U.S. Elections* (Washington, D.C.: Congressional Quarterly Press, 1975), 483-509.

[4]Compiled from the official *Congressional Directory*, 2d session, Congresses 79-94; and in part from Leon Freidman and Fred L. Israel, eds., *The Justices of the United States Supreme Court 1789-1969: Their Lives and Major Opinions* (New York: Chelsea House in Association with Bowker, 1969-1978), 4: 3232-35.

A number of the factors contributing to House turnover have been assessed already in political science journals. An emphasis has been on relatively recent variables, such as vanishing marginals, declining party competitiveness since 1950, modern advantages of incumbency, and the congressman's increasing orientation to bureaucratic tasks.[5]

As for the ascendancy of dissimilar norms in past generations, opinions and principles are obscure influences to measure. Yet they lie within the sphere of political science, for conceptual precepts secure obedience both within the governmental hierarchy and among the citizenry. "Ideas are, in truth, forces."[6]

One such force was the principle of rotation in office. George Mason of Virginia, one of the more influential Founders, held that, "Nothing is so essential to the preservation of a republican government as a periodic

---

[5]Notable recent studies not cited elsewhere in this chapter include the following: H. Douglas Price, "The Congressional Career Then and Now," in *Congressional Behavior,* ed. Nelson W. Polsby (New York: Random House, 1971), 14-27; H. Douglas Price, "Congress and the Evolution of Legislative 'Professionalism'," in *Congress in Change,* ed. Norman J. Ornstein (New York: Praeger Publishers, 1975), 2-23; Morris P. Fiorina, "The Case of the Vanishing Marginals: The Bureaucracy Did It," *American Political Science Review* 71 (1977): 177-81; John A. Ferejohn, "On the Decline of Competition in Congressional Elections," *American Political Science Review* 71 (1977): 166-76; Richard G. Hutcheson III, "The Internal Effect of Incumbency and Two-Party Politics: Elections to the House of Representatives from the South, 1952-74," *American Political Science Review* 69 (1975): 1399-1401; Walter Dean Burnham, "American Politics in the 1970's," in *The American Party Systems,* 2d ed., ed. William Chambers and Walter Burnham (New York: Oxford University Press, 1975), 317-40; David R. Mayhew, "Congressional Elections: The Case of the Vanishing Marginals," *Polity* 6 (Spring 1974): 295-317; Albert D. Cover, "One Good Term Deserves Another: The Advantage of Incumbency in Congressional Elections," *American Journal of Political Science* 21 (1977): 523-41; Robert S. Erickson, "The Advantages of Incumbency in Congressional Elections," *Polity* 3 (Spring 1971): 395-405. For a rebuttal to the latter and Erickson's reply see *Polity* 4 (Summer 1972): 523-29.

[6]Quotation from, Henry James, *Charles W. Eliot,* 2 vols. (Boston: Houghton Mifflin Company, 1930), 1:235. On ideas and their effect on history see, Allan Nevins, *The Gateway to History*, revised paperback edition (Garden City, N.Y.: Doubleday & Company, Inc., 1938, 1962), 261-62.

rotation."[7] This point of view was popular in the United States for a century or more and ought not to be ignored for its direct effect on Congress or conversely for the absence of its impetus when, as today, the body politic attributes more utility to tenure.

A difficulty for scholars has been the paucity of data on congressional elections that antedate the 1950s. Although two studies have compiled data on percentage of first-termers per House, as well as average tenure per Congress since 1789,[8] neither statistic reveals the chief components in turnover—i.e., congressmen withdrawing from contention before the general elections and defeats of incumbents at the polls.

To discover these components became practical after the publication of *Congressional Quarterly's Guide to U.S. Elections* (1975). Employing this source of raw data in 1977, Samuel Kernell's useful compilations of pre-election withdrawals concentrated on five selected decades, so chosen chronologically as to confine his quantitative analysis to the downward side of the 19th century trend in withdrawals.[9] The earlier rising portion of the trend is, I believe, indispensable to a balanced study of rotation. Nor did Kernell afford much attention to electoral defeats, which relate to public opinion on rotation more directly than withdrawals.

The present effort takes a comprehensive approach and breaks down the House turnover into withdrawals of incumbents, and percentage of incumbents defeated at the polls, during the entire century and a half, 1824-1976.

First, the matter under investigation needs an *ad hoc* definition. For the purposes of this chapter turnover is simply change in House membership for any reason, public or private, whereas the rotation implies departure of

---

[7]Jonathan Eliot, ed., *The Debates in the Several State Conventions on Adoption of the Federal Constitution*, 5 vols. (Washington, D.C.: Government Printing Office, 1836), 3:485.

[8]Stuart A. Rice, *Quantitative Methods*, 296-97; Nelson W. Polsby, "The Institutionalization of the U.S. House of Representatives," *American Political Science Review* 62 (1968): 146, tables 1 and 2; Morris P. Fiorina, David W. Rohde, and Peter Wissel, "Historical Change in House Turnover," in *Congress in Change*, ed. Norman J. Ornstein (New York: Praeger Publishers, 1975), 26.

[9]Samuel Kernell, "Toward Understanding 19th Century Congressional Careers: Ambition, Competition, and Rotation," *American Journal of Political Science* 21 (1977): 669-93.

incumbent congressmen because of political and/or social aversion to long tenure in office.

This study will not be confined to an historical enforcement of rotation in constant and mechanistic ways, such as Kernell's investigation of strict two-term customs in nominating conventions. Instead, rotation is here defined as the turnover resulting from an idea, a normative judgment, an evaluation—specifically the negative evaluation in America of congressional careerism. This socio-political bias reinforced whatever political obstacles a post-1789 incumbent faced and represented a debit in the equation for elective careers. The debit was potentially decisive at various stages of an individual's career and in a number of ways: for example through peer group pressures, in the nominating conventions, or at the polls.

Of course evidence of the influence of an idea or principle must necessarily be circumstantial, in that the multitude of 19th-century incumbents, nominators, and voters cannot be surveyed as to motives. Yet insofar as the wax and wane of rotation's popularity, as indicated by testimonial evidence—contemporary books, newspapers, letters, etc.—meshes chronologically with the quantitative data; one has to think that so fundamental a reevaluation by the body politic as to whether tenure is an asset or a liability, must indeed have been a significant factor in contemporaneous renominations and reelections.

I. ROTATION BEFORE 1824

A brief look at rotation in office during the initial half-century of independence will serve to preface and put into perspective the analysis of rotation norms after 1824.

For some 15 years until the adoption of the U.S. Constitution America was a debating ground as to governmental forms. The educated class studied ancient constitutions and cited them as relevant to the American experiment. Prior to the first century B.C. the polis generally rotated its officials annually; notable were Athens, Sparta, and republican Rome.[10]

---

[10]Aristotle, *Constitution of Athens* 4.3, 46.1, 62.3; Charles Hignett, *A History of the Athenian Constitution* (Oxford: Clarendon Press, 1958), 153, 237-44; A. H. M. Jones, *Sparta* (Oxford: Basil Blackwell, 1967), 26; Livy, *History of Rome* VII 42.2, X 13.8, XXVII 6.6; *Periochae* LVI; Cicero De Legibus III 3.7-9; Plutarch

Also the Middle Ages and Italian Renaissance saw a number of city-states in northern Italy employ rotation extensively in the highest political offices. Florence did so for centuries, with interludes,[11] and Venice for more than 600 years without interruption until the Napoleonic conquest.[12] Americans studied also the theory behind rotation in office, as articulated during antiquity by Aristotle,[13] and in the early modern period by James Harrington, the author of *Oceania*.[14]

> In January, 1776, John Adams assessed American opinion on the eve of Independence: "A rotation of all offices, as well as of representatives and counsellors, has many advocates, and is contended for with many plausible arguments. . . . These persons may be allowed to serve for three years, and then be excluded three years, or for any longer or shorter term."[15]

By 1787 the triennial rotation of the Continental Congress had been six years in force under the Articles of Confederation. When Governor Edmund Randolph read the Virginia Plan during the second week of the Constitutional convention, it provided for exit, after a single term, of all incumbents in the lower chamber of the national legislature.[16] But during the fourth week the convention rejected the ban on consecutive terms.[17] No doubt, the mandatory rotation had been discredited somewhat by association with the

---

Gaius Marius 12.1; Leon Pol Homo, *Roman Political Institutions from City to State* (New York: Alfred A. Knopf, 1929), 160-61.

[11]Ferdinand Schevill, *History of Florence* (New York: Harcourt, Brace and Company, 1936), 67, 154, 162, 209-10; Bella Duffy, *The Tuscan Republics* (New York: G. P. Putnam's Sons, 1898), 105.

[12]Frederick C. Lane, *Venice, A Maritime Republic* (Baltimore: The John Hopkins University Press, 1973), 96-97, 100, 116, 251, 257, 392, 428-29.

[13]Aristotle, *The Politics* III 4.5-7, VI 1.6, 8.

[14]James Harrington, *The Oceania and Other Works of James Harrington . . .*, ed. John Toland (London: A. Miller, 1747), 54-57, 124-25, 140, 161, 303-23, 500, 504, 523, 623-24, 629, 632.

[15]John Adams, *The Life and Works of John Adams*, ed. Charles Francis Adams, 10 vols. (Boston: Charles C. Little and James Brown, 1851), 4:197-98.

[16]Max Farrand, ed., *The Records of the Federal Convention of 1787*, 4 vols. (New Haven: Yale University Press, 1911), 1:20, resolution 4.

[17]*Ibid.*, vol. 1, entries for June 12.

Confederation. The convention delegates defeated also the various plans to ban or restrict reelection in the presidency.

Efforts toward a rotation amendment continued for a year or two after the convention of 1787. Leading advocates included George Mason, Thomas Jefferson, and Richard Henry Lee.[18] Their insistence on constitutional limitation of tenure proved fruitless, but the philosophical objections to perpetuity in office continued well into the future and operated on an extraconstitutional basis.

For the years 1789-1823, good data on withdrawals and electoral defeats are not available, and no quantitative analysis of rotation in that generation will be attempted here. James Young's *The Washington Community, 1800-1828,* is an important source for the general distrust of power in that period.[19] Also some normative writings before 1824 are illustrative. According to one early congressman, continuous reelections were perilous because in time "the very best men among us become more or less impressed with opinions not comfortable to that of the people."[20] An 1822 editorial in the influential Niles *Weekly Register* supports this reasoning, because in politics "the mind gradually becomes callous of wrong."[21] In the same year an article in the *Richmond Enquirer*, entitled "Rotation in Office," argues that lengthy tenure in Congress promotes usurpation of power from the states and the people; and the article contends that the "long cherished" principle of rotation has been impressed on the republican mind "by a kind of intuitive impulse, unassailable to argument or authority."[22]

---

[18]Jonathan Eliot, *Debates* 3:485; Thomas Jefferson, *Papers* 12:440, 13:490; Richard Henry Lee, *An additional number of Letters from the Federal Farmer to the Republican* IX 2.

[19]James S. Young, *The Washington Community, 1800-1828* (New York: Columbia University Press, 1966), 51-52, 55-57, 59-61, 64, 145.

[20]Hezekia Niles, "Rotation in Office," *Niles Weekly Register* 23 (November 16, 1822), 162.

[21]*Ibid.*

[22]*Richmond Enquirer*, November 8, 1822, 3.

II. INCUMBENT DEFEATS IN GENERAL
ELECTIONS, 1824-1976

The rotation impulse—for some voters intuitive, for others theoretically developed—is implied in the electoral defeats after 1824. The basic measure will be the percent of incumbent congressmen standing for reelection who lose at the polls. The analytical procedure will be to present indications of rotation's influence on 19th-century voting patterns and then to advance further evidence against two plausible objections. The general thesis is that the relatively high levels of incumbent defeats before the 20th century, especially for the more senior incumbents, and the lower loss rates since, are related to the wax and wane of the rotation principle as a conceptual force.

Some quantitative evidence is summarized in Table 1.[23]

First, in terms of time series data, changing attitudes toward long tenure in office should logically have the least effect on freshmen defeats. A freshman seeking reelection would be less likely than say a sophomore, to gain or lose votes from comparison with the nonincumbent challenger's newcomer status. And indeed the break down (in Table 1) of the incumbent defeats into freshmen *vis-à-vis* the more senior congressmen, shows relatively moderate time series fluctuations in the defeat rates for freshmen. During the century and a third, 1824-1960, average defeats of freshmen incumbents stay between 20 and 30 percent inclusive,[24] with as recent a

---

[23]The reader will note the exclusion from Table 1 of defeat rates for southern congressmen. The only portions of data for which the percentage of defeats in the South equals or exceeds that of the rest of the nation are the years 1824-37 and 1866-76 (Reconstruction). One party dominance shifted the action to the nominating stage after Reconstruction and eventually reduced general election defeats in the South to the vicinity of zero percent. The inclusion of such data only distorts the picture of what is taking place in the meaningful general elections, and for the sake of uniformity and simplicity the 11 states of the secession are excluded from the entirety of the 1824-1976 analysis of defeats.

[24]The range between 20 percent and 30 percent in freshmen defeats represents the long-term average. The biennial fluctuations for the period 1824-1960 are much wider, of course, ranging from 10 percent to 51 percent, as voters reacted to short term issues.

Table 1. *Percentage of Incumbent Candidates, Outside the South, Defeated in General Elections: Relative Spread between Freshmen and Rest of Incumbent Field*

Election Years	Average % defeated		Ratio of columns 2 to 3
	Frosh	2+ termers	
1824-37	20	19	1.1 to 1
1838-65	30	23	1.3 to 1
1866-96	25	18	1.4 to 1
1898-32	23	11	2.1 to 1
1934-48	28	11	2.5 to 1
1950-60	20	5.4	3.7 to 1
1962-76	12	5.6	2.1 to 1

Source: Appendix II

period as 1934-48 having a freshman defeat rate of 28 percent. Only since 1960 has the long-term rate for freshmen fallen below 20 percent.

Second using the relatively constant freshman rate as a reference point in time series, the rest of the incumbent field (hereafter signified "2+ termers" for sophomores and up) can be compared historically for shifting voter preferences respecting tenure. The effect of voter adherence to rotation norms should be to narrow the gap between the "ceiling" defeat rate of freshmen and the rate for 2+ termers. Conversely, when rotation declines and voters attribute more value to experience, the spread between freshmen and 2+ termers should widen.

As indicated by the ratios in Table 1, the gap as of the first third of the 20th century reached a then record width and continued to widen further until 1960. If as suggested by this data, the about face in public thinking took place on the eve of the turn of the century, then it would tentatively seem that the movement for a professional civil service and the nation's clear rejection of rotation in appointive federal office after 1883, was the vanguard by not many years of the equivalent trend for the office of congressman.

That the great decline of rotation's popularity with voters took place shortly before 1900 is consistent with the watershed character of the last two decades of the 19th century. Basic shifts in the American mode of life included urbanization, the industrial revolution, and the end of the frontier.[25] These fundamental changes accelerated tremendously from 1880 to 1900 and, accompanied by the economic and political shocks of 1893-96, they created a political climate very different than the milieu in which rotation had flourished.

The preliminary conclusions are as follows: (1) After 1824 public favor for rotation in office—as a defined principle and/or simply an intuitive impulse to throw the rascals out—worked to retard what superiority in polling strength 2+ termers enjoyed as compared to freshmen congressmen. (2) Near 1900 a counter trend in public evaluation of long tenure in office promoted substantially wider spreads in reelection rates between freshmen and 2+ termers.

Objection One. The 2+ field has varied by composition. In 1838-65 only 17 percent of the 2+ candidates consisted of 4+ termers. as compared with 50 percent during 1906-32. By 1950-76 two-thirds of the 2+ field consisted of 4+ termers. This aging of the nonfreshmen is more significant than shifting voter preference as a factor in the declining 2+ termer defeat rate.

Answer. In terms of political advantage at the polls, the accumulation of incumbency yields minimal rates of return after the sophomore term. Table 2's breakdown of 2+ data into rates for 2, 3, and 4+ termers, reveals that 20th-century incumbents accrue most of their polling power during the second term. Between 1906 and 1960 the 4+ termers performed within two percentage points of sophomores.

In addition, time series comparisons within the respective classes—within the middle columns in Table 2—where accumulation of tenure is equal over time, show a chronological decline that is quite large. The rate's downward trend would seem to derive from the electorate's changing

---

[25]Frederick Jackson Turner, *The Frontier in American History* (New York: Henry Holt and Company, 1953), Chapter 1. Reprint of paper presented to the American Historical Association, 1893.

Table 2. *Percentage of Incumbent Candidates, Outside the South, Defeated in General Elections: Breakdown by Terms of House Service*

Election Years	Terms served by incumbents			
	1	2	3	4+
1838-65	30	25	19	19
1906-32	24	13	13	11
1934-48	28	10	13	10
1950-60	20	7.6	3.1	5.3
1962-76	12	9.0	5.1	4.8

Source: Appendix II

evaluation of the tenure for the class in question. Sophomores average 25 percent defeats about mid 19th century and 7.6 percent defeats near mid 20th century. The three-termers drop from 19 percent to 3.1 percent during the same period.

The continuing decline of defeats during the 20th century is not of course due to the abandonment of antitenure attitudes as such, for rotation norms were disregarded early in the century. As rotation's receding popularity was a gradual ebb terminating about 1900, so did the subsequent flow of its antithesis, the principle of expertise, gradually accrue. The negation of socio-political bias against careerism meant that long tenure was tolerable, not that it was at once affirmed enthusiastically in 1900. Increasingly, the 20th century saw professionalism insisted upon in virtually every occupational field, including politics. This model derived from everyday observation would naturally be reflected in voter preferences, which is consistent with the steady increase until 1960 in rates of reelection for 2, 3, and 4+ termers.

Objection two. The data can be explained better in terms of party competitiveness. In competitive eras, defeats would be spread more evenly according to seniority; whereas eras of sectionalism would see safe careers

(2+ termers) in the safe districts, with freshmen coring from the remaining competitive districts where defeat rates are high.

Answer. Amongst every class of incumbents, 19th-century withdrawals were numerous; so that freshmen were well represented, as an aftermath of seniors withdrawing, even in districts that had little party turnover. It is noteworthy that the period 1824-34, one of the most sectionalistic eras ever, saw the electoral defeat rates virtually identical for freshmen and 2+ termers.

Second, the period 1934-48, described by E. E. Schattschneider as competitive in all the states outside the South,[26] saw the gap in defeat rates between freshmen and 2+ termers continue to widen relative to the earlier gap during the sectionalistic fourth-party system. Indeed, the rate for 3 termers remained the same as during the quarter century prior, and sophomores actually incurred defeats at a lower rate than before; yet the freshman defeat rate rose substantially in response to the more competitive situation. The party competitiveness thesis does not explain why the rate for 2+ termers failed to respond upward as well. Changing voting habits do explain it: the electorate's increasing preference for 2+ term tenure was strong enough to cancel out the conducement to defeats inherent in party competitiveness.

Third, the long-term decline in the defeat rates for 2, 3, and 4+ termers spans four-party systems; it is too consistently in decline to derive only from competitiveness, which fluctuates up and down more than once over the same period.

To sum up, in 19th-century House elections, the rotation idea was influential enough in public thinking not to quash but certainly to retard the advantage accruing to the accumulation of incumbency. The northern electorate of 1838-65 defeated 4+ termers at the relatively high rate of 19 percent (more frequently than 20th-century voters have turned out sophomores—11 percent). Second, popular loyalty to the principle of rotation never demanded that 19th-century voters defeat a majority of the

---

[26]E. E. Schattschneider, "United States: The Functional Approach to Party Government," in *Modern Political Parties,* ed. Sigmund Neumann (Chicago: The University of Chicago Press, 1956), 208; Walter Dean Burnham, "Party Systems and the Political Process," in *The American Party Systems*, ed. William Chambers and Walter Dean Burnham, 302.

incumbent candidates; because, as we shall see, so many congressmen withdrew at the nomination stage that rapid turnover in the House was a certainty, even had the voters reelected every incumbent on the ballot. The rotation principle was a significant check to reelection if it simply dulled or nullified the natural weapon of every incumbent—his propaganda appeal on the basis of experience in Congress.

Third, that the mid 19th-century 4+ termer enjoyed a moderately better chance at the polls than the freshman or sophomore incumbents of his day can be attributed in part to the selectivity at the nominating stage, where to survive for four terms must have required exceptional skill in the political arena.[27] A major reason the 4+ termer did somewhat better in general elections was apparently that it took shrewder politicians just to achieve four renominations.

Finally, it is safe to say that especially during the era from the second Adams to Appomattox, 1824-65, the occupancy of a seat in Congress for several terms did not greatly impress voters. The incumbent's experience in the House was disregarded by many citizens, was feared by others as conducive to an aristocracy of officeholders,[28] or was deemed noxious for the incumbents themselves because "power is too apt to turn the head."[29]

III. WITHDRAWALS, 1824-1976

Withdrawal of incumbents prior to the general elections was much the largest component in House turnover. For the seven decades 1824-96, an average of 35 percent of the House withdrew from the running before the general elections, or about two-thirds of the average turnover from all causes (51 percent). Furthermore, as indicated in Figure A, the trend in withdrawals was steeply up between 1824 and mid century, was erratic for a period of 14 years that included the Civil War, and was sharply down

---

[27]So few congressmen won four renominations during the years 1838-65 that the incumbent candidates with four successive terms or more averaged a mere 2.9 percent of their expiring House memberships.

[28]James Bryce, *The American Commonwealth*, 3d ed., 2 vols. (New York: The MacMillan Company, 1907), 2:241; Edwin L. Godkin, in *Cyclopaedia of Political Science*, 3 vols., ed. John J. Laylor (New York: Charles E. Merrill & Co., 1890), 3:19.

[29]*Richmond Enquirer*, November 12, 1822, 3.

between 1868 and 1898—a trend that matches chronologically the wax and wane of the spoils form of rotation, introduced by the Jacksonians.

In 1829, in his first address to Congress, President Andrew Jackson declared that rotation in office "constitutes a leading principle in the republican creed."[30] The seventh president went on during his eight years, to enforce an unprecedented turnover in the executive bureaucracy. Following this extension of the spoils system to the federal level came a fundamental change in how Americans viewed U.S. government. For more than half a century, as will be shown, the idea that federal offices were spoils to be spread around among the party faithful had a significant effect not only on appointive places, but also on nominations for the elective seats in Congress.

During the years after Jackson, 1838-53, the rate of withdrawal in non-southern states averaged 45 percent among freshmen congressmen, 61 percent among sophomores, and 42 percent among 3+ termers. The configuration by class in rates of withdrawal continues to show a bias toward the sophomores through the 1890s according to Kernell's figures.[31] In volume, the great bulk of the withdrawals at mid century accrued to the freshmen, as by far the largest class in the House.

The role of rotation in promoting these withdrawals is touched upon by the *New York Statesman* in 1824. The newspaper ascribes many or "perhaps most" of the turnover in the state's congressional delegation to, "an arrangement, by which it is stipulated, that, after a given time, one aspirant for office is to succeed another."[32]

Such arrangements took principally two forms during the 19th century: (1) agreements between competitors in a nominating convention that the incumbent, normally after one or two terms of service, shall then retire and aid the nomination of his nearest rival; (2) a custom known as the claim of locality, whereby the different geographical sections of the congressional

---

[30]James D. Richardson, ed., *A Compilation of the Messages and Papers of the Presidents*, 10 vols. (Washington, D.C.: Government Printing Office, 1896-99), 2:448-49.

[31]Samuel Kernell, "Toward Understanding 19th Century Congressional Careers: Ambition, Competition, and Rotation," *American Political Science Review* 21 (1977): 669-93, especially Figure 2, 687.

[32]Quoted in *Niles Weekly Register* 27:217.

district furnished the party's candidate in turn.[33] The former case, agreements between competitors, found its most favorable milieu in the district conventions, which became increasingly standard nominating machinery after the Jacksonian Revolution began. More than in state legislative caucuses or statewide conventions, the local leaders in district conventions held sway and could reach and enforce agreements to pass the seat around among themselves.

A case in point was Illinois' seventh congressional district, where Abraham Lincoln resided, and where the Whigs adopted the convention system in 1843. Lincoln's associates, Nicolay and Hay, portray the setting:

> The Sangammon district was the one which the Whigs of Illinois had apparently the best prospect of carrying, and it was full of able and ambitious men, who were nominated successively for the only place which gave them the opportunity of playing a part in the national theatre at Washington.[34]

In 1846 a meeting by the Whigs of the Athena precinct is notable for moving the nomination of Lincoln with the following whereas clause: "our present Representative, Hon. E. D. Baker, recognizing the principle of 'rotation in office,' has generously declined a reelection."[35] However, the predecessor of Baker proved less cooperative. Former Rep. Hardin declared his candidacy against Lincoln, waged a hot contest, and moved Lincoln to remind Hardin by letter of an agreement three years earlier, between themselves and Baker, that none of the three—Hardin, Baker, Lincoln—was to be a candidate out of his turn.[36] Hardin soon withdrew his candidacy,[37]

---

[33]Frederick W. Dallinger, *Nominations for Elective Office in the United States* (New York: Longmans, Green, and Co., 1897), 88-89; Laurence N. Powell, "Rejected Republican Incumbents in the 1866 Congressional Nominating Conventions," *Civil War History* 19 (1973): 228-33.

[34]John G. Nicolay and John Hay, *Abraham Lincoln: A History*, 10 vols. (New York: The Century Co., 1890), 1:289.

[35]*Lacon Illinois Gazette*, February 7, 1846, 2.

[36]In 1843 the Whigs of the seventh (Sangammon) district nominated General John Hardin for Congress. Also the convention approved, 19 to 14, delegate Abraham Lincoln's motion limiting Hardin to a single term and designating Edward D. Baker as the Whig candidate for the subsequent term. *Lacon Illinois*

and in the district convention Lincoln's[38] nomination was without opposition.[39]

Lincoln exited the House by the same principle. During the first year of his single term in Congress he wrote his law partner that political support notwithstanding, he would not run for reelection, excepting no other Whig came forward, because "to enter myself as a competitor of another, or to authorize anyone so to enter me, is what my word and honor forbid."[40] The Whig nomination went in 1848 to Steven Logan, who had nominated Lincoln in the previous district convention.[41]

Geographic rotation, or the claim of locality, operated somewhat differently from the rotation among rivals like Baker, Lincoln, and Logan, who all resided in the city of Springfield. As Nicolay and Hay observed with some exaggeration: "To ask in a nominating convention who is best qualified for service in Congress is always regarded as an impertinence; but the question 'what county in the district has had the Congressman oftenest' is always considered in order."[42] Also an article in the *Christian Examiner*, September 1869, states that,

> [T]here is a constant temptation, in a district made up of an aggregation of counties or towns, to pass the offices round from town to town, or county, to another; each claiming in its turn the honor of furnishing the member.[43]

Gazette, February 14, 1846, 2.

[37]Abraham Lincoln, *The Collected Works of Abraham Lincoln*, ed. Roy P. Basler, 10 vols. (New Brunswick, N.J.: Rutgers University Press, 1953), 1:361. Letter to John Hardin, February 7, 1846.

[38]*Lacon Illinois Gazette*, February 28, 1846, 2.

[39]John G. Nicolay and John Hay, *A History* 1:245.

[40]Roy P. Basler, *Works of Lincoln* 1:430-31. Letter to William Herndon, January 8, 1848.

[41]John G. Nicolay and John Hay, *A History* 1:245.

[42]*Ibid.*, 1:290.

[43]W. F. Allen, "The Caucus System in the United States," *The Christian Examiner* 87 (September 1869), 148.

In 1866 just such a system characterized New York State according to Horace Greeley.[44]

The chronology of the gradual eclipse of nomination rotation is perhaps best seen in the declining trend line for withdrawals that is steepest for the 30 years, 1868-98. Testimonial evidence is also indicative. Rotation in the House was still strong enough when James Bryce visited America in the 1870s and 1880s that he found: "So far from its being, as in England, a reason for re-electing a man that he has been a member already, it is a reason for passing him by, and giving somebody else a turn."[45] And as late as July 1896, Frederick W. Dallinger wrote that intraparty agreements among rivals to rotate the nomination occurred "often," while in other districts geographic rotation was "customary."[46] It was, however, but the remnants of these practices that gave way to direct primaries between 1903 and 1915.[47]

The theory of withdrawals. A separate aspect of nomination rotation was the normative justification, i.e., the principle, or at least the appearance of principle, to embellish the practice. As conceptually understood rotation was, according to Bryce, the philosophical adjunct without which the country would never have let the politicians rivet the spoils system to the civil service,[48] so did the same philosophy lift the intraparty machinations for sharing seats in Congress to a level of respectability impossible if the practice were unadorned.

Until the rise of the Jacksonians, the principle of rotation at the federal level was pretty much limited to the connotation it had held since the Revolution—that of the antipower attitudes documented in chapter three of the award winning book by James Young.[49] The tendency to look askance at political power was so ingrained into American culture, says Young, that even the officeholders themselves perceived their occupations in a

---

[44]Laurence N. Powell, "Rejected Republican Incumbents," 236, footnote 109.

[45]James Bryce, *The American Commonwealth*, 2d ed., 2 vols. (New York: Macmillan and Co., 1891), 1:192. (1:195-96 in 3d ed., but the phrase "as in England" is omitted.)

[46]Frederick W. Dallinger, *Nominations*, 88-89.

[47]C. E. Merriam and L. Overacker, *Primary Elections* (Chicago: University of Chicago Press, 1928), 61-63.

[48]James Bryce, *American Commonwealth*, 3d ed., 2:133.

[49]James S. Young, *The Washington Community, 1800-1828.*

disparaging light.[50] A widespread conviction was articulated by James Fenimore Cooper in 1838, ". . . contact with the affairs of state is one of the most corrupting of the influences to which men are exposed."[51] Half a century earlier the president of the Continental Congress, R. H. Lee, had written to Samuel Adams: "The fact is, that power poisons the mind of its possessor. . . . "[52]

The Jacksonians mixed this original connotation to rotation with an entirely new meaning. For both mayor parties rotation in office came to embrace the doctrine of taking turns in the distribution of prizes. More than once in his quest for the Whig nomination to Congress Lincoln employed the slogan, "turnabout is fair play."[53] By fair play he referred not to the Youngian antipower notions but to the contest for the prize of office.[54]

During the second quarter of the 19th century the antipathy to power (which was held to be in the best interests of the country) and the normative innovations of the Jacksonians (which played to the self interest of local leaders) were coupled under one philosophical heading called rotation in office. Apparently the combination of connotations and motives redoubled the impetus to nomination rotation and promoted a steep rise in incumbent withdrawals. By mid century close to half the House membership per term agreed, either voluntarily or by party push, not to seek reelection.

That the principle of rotation was the deciding factor or at least a major contributor to the rise in withdrawals, is yet more credible in that the post-bellum decline in the popularity of the spoils principle parallelled the downward trend in the withdrawal rate. According to Professor Carl Russell Fish the decline of rotation in the civil service dates from 1865 when

---

[50]*Ibid.*, 51-52, 59-61, 64, 145.

[51]James Fenimore Cooper, *The American Democrat* (New York: Alfred A. Knopf, 1931), 52.

[52]Richard Henry Lee, *The Letters of Richard Henry Lee*, ed. James C. Ballagh, 2 vols. (New York: The Macmillan Company, 1914), 2:344, March 14, 1785.

[53]Roy P. Basler, ed., *Works of Lincoln* 1:359. Letter to N. J. Rockwell, January 21, 1846. Also 1:361.

[54]By Lincoln's time the spoils principle had become so acceptable to Whigs as well as the Democrats, that a Whig writer could boldly oppose the nomination of a fellow Whig and former congressman on the following grounds: "we maintain that it is Mr. Lincoln's turn to 'rotate' into congress, that his 'turn' has come." *Lacon Illinois Gazette*, February 14, 1846, 2, column 5.

President Lincoln refused to enforce rotation in the appointive offices under his jurisdiction.[55] Later that year Rep. Thomas Allen Jenckes introduced his first civil service reform bill, which the House would vote down by a narrow margin. In defeat the Jenckes reform bill became the springboard of a great national debate. The 1872 Democratic party platform heralded civil service reform as "one of the most pressing necessities of the hour," while the Republican platform of the same year advocated reforms to "make honesty, efficiency and fidelity the essential qualifications for public positions, without practically creating a life-tenure of office."[56] During the years 1872-92, every platform of the two mayor parties contained strong planks for civil service reform. The Republican proviso against a life tenure of office vanished after 1872. Meanwhile the country's newspapers and periodical literature had been replete with articles and editorials supporting the reformers from Jenckes onward. The postbellum generation underwent, in short, something of a revolution in the prevailing attitudes toward career government service. Careerism was transformed in leading minds from a vice to a virtue, and the effects of this conceptual revolution could not but spill over into the sphere of elective office.

The idea of rotation was called further into question after 1865 by at least two basic social changes. (1) Post-Civil War America witnessed a growing ascendancy of cosmopolitan over local life. Support for spoils was rooted in the localities, and the declining influence of counties and towns hastened the eclipse of nomination rotation.[57] (2) The postbellum 19th century saw a shift in the balance of power to the business class, where

---

[55]Carl Russell Fish, *The Civil Service and the Patronage* (New York: Longmans, Green, and Co., 1905), 172. Contemporary accounts also cite as a turning point the Civil War *per se*. According to an 1868 article, it mattered less how officialdom exercised its functions prior to the war, "for the Government was seen rather than felt, it was an idea rather than a fact. All this changed with the rebellion. . . . " *Nation* 6 (May 28, 1868), 425.

[56]Kirk H. Porter and Bruce Johnson, ed., *National Party Platforms, 1840-1960*, 2d ed. (Urbana: University of Illinois Press, 1961), 42, 47.

[57]Samuel P. Hays, "Political Parties and the Community-Society Continuum," 172-73, 177; and Walter Dean Burnham, "Party Systems and the Political Process," 284, both works in *Party Systems*, ed. William Chambers and Walter Dean Burnham; Laurence N. Powell, "Rejected Republican Incumbents," 236-37.

professionalism and careerism were increasingly the standard. In turn, U.S. government began to reflect the methods and manner of the ruling industrial elite.[58] Big business was then both novel and awesome in its success, and this formidable model dissented from the antipower attitudes described by Young. In short, the industrial revolution in America contained elements hostile both to the spoils principle and to the older norms concerning the perils of long tenure in power.

To sum up: The long-term fluctuations in the quantitative phenomena of withdrawals by congressmen were related to whether the politicians and voters in the nation regarded careerism as good or evil, fair or unfair, expedient or inopportune. When these normative judgments were reversed, a revolution in basic political values had transpired, and a major transformation of Congress ensued.

The chronology of such a revolution in ideas is more broad brush than for the practices. As late as 1889 Frederic Whitridge wrote in *Political Science Quarterly* that many Americans regarded the idea of rotation in office as a "shibboleth" by which their neighbor's democracy might be tested. But by 1904 Professor Fish was writing in the past tense about "the days of rotation."[59]

It may well be that Youngian-like misgivings about prolongation in office, as expressed by the electorate, outlasted intraparty support for the spoils principle as manifested in withdrawals. For a quarter century before the economic depression of 1893-97, incumbent withdrawals had been in steep decline, whereas at the polls incumbent defeat rates had yet to fall substantially. Neither did the gap in electoral defeat rates between freshmen and 2+ termers widen appreciably until the late 1890s.

---

[58]Samuel P. Hays, *ibid.*, 177-78; C. R. Fish, *Civil Service*, 233, 245; Edwin L. Godkin, *Cyclopaedia of Political Science* 3:24.

[59]Frederick W. Whitridge, "Rotation in Office," *Political Science Quarterly* 4 (1889): 281, 294; C. R. Fish, *Civil Service*, 36-37. Both Whitridge and Fish refer principally to rotation in the civil service, but rotation had similar apologies and conceptual support wherever applied. Rotation in appointive vs. elective office was a fairly subtle distinction, and the declining popularity of both applications seems to have been closely associated.

IV. ROTATION RELATIVE TO AMBITION AND COMPETITION IN THE 19TH CENTURY

Of course other variables than rotation contributed to the component trends in turnover. T. Richard Witmer wrote in 1964 that a "labyrinth of factors" accounted for the increase in survivability in the House.[60] One factor, institutionalization of the House internally, as elucidated by Nelson W. Polsby,[61] became a factor quite late in the 19th century or early in the 20th. Two variables that were significant throughout the 19th century—ambition and party competition—bear on the contemporary importance of rotation.

In 1977 Samuel Kernell asserted that nomination rotation did serve as a "significant impediment" to career development, but that it was of third-rate importance behind (1) the ambition of incumbents for House careers, and (2) interparty competition as manifested in defeat at the polls.[62] Kernell's analysis undervalues rotation, I find, in at least four respects.

First, as established above in section II, rotation was a factor in 19th-century electoral defeats. Kernell makes the assumption that changing defeat rates at the polls were due almost exclusively to party competitiveness.

Second, rotation is causally interrelated to ambition, because the attractiveness of the job—hence ambition—was linked culturally to whether prolongation in office was deemed good, neutral, or evil by contemporary society and peers.

Third, the effect of interparty competition on withdrawals was also causally interrelated to rotation. The mayor parties came to regard nominations for the House as "salary" due their leading troops.[63] Making good on this payroll, through rotation in nominations, helped keep the intrastate party machinery in fighting trim. And of course to win the numerous state and local offices, discipline in the party ranks was more

---

[60]T. Richard Witmer, "The Aging of the House," *Political Science Quarterly* 79 (1964): 527-28.

[61]Nelson W. Polsby, "The Institutionalization of the U.S. House of Representatives," 144-68.

[62]Samuel Kernell, "Ambition, Competition, and Rotation," 688-90.

[63]James Bryce, *American Commonwealth*, 3d ed., 2:133.

important, especially with stiff competition, than the modest returns to the party expectable from incumbent renominations to the U.S. House.

Had the custom of nomination rotation not existed, competition would have placed the expediency from the state and local party's perspective on renominating incumbents as the stronger candidates. The spoils principle shifted the locus of expediency to withdrawals, so as to spread the pay-offs as widely as possible. This intraparty motive was intensified by interparty competition. Since competition called for party discipline, which required more attention to the rotations payroll, competition and the nomination rotation were causally interrelated.

Fourth, Kernell's methodology in estimating the effect of rotation on House turnover is demonstrably invalid for the antebellum period, when rotation was at full tide. To determine the percent of all careers ended by rotation, Kernell simply subtracts the percent of sophomores renominated from the percent of freshmen renominated, on the assumption that a two-term limit was so much the prevailing form in nominating conventions that rotation was not, on average, conducive to withdrawals by first-termers.[64] This methodology leads Kernell to conclude that rotation terminated no more than four percent of all House careers after 1854.

An examination in Table 3 of the three largest state delegations in the House during the 10 elections of 1838-57 is particularly useful because it is possible to ignore the factor of ambition—assuming that at this point in time, the House was more or less equally attractive to incumbent congressmen from New York, Pennsylvania, and Ohio. A fourth state, Massachusetts, is not included in the analysis, but appears in Table 3 for reference, as the northern state with the lowest withdrawal rate.

Table 3 as well as testimonial evidence indicates that during the 10 elections covered, New York was the leading state in commitment to rotation in office. At that time the Albany Regency so dominated Democratic politics in the Empire State that, according to Jabez Hammond, the Regency settled "all questions in relation to the selection of candidates for elective office."[65] The Regency was led by Martin Van Buren, William

---

[64]Samuel Kernell, "Ambition, Competition, and Rotation," 688.

[65]Jabez D. Hammond, *The History of Political Parties in the State of New-York*, 3 vols. (Cooperstown, N.Y.: H. & E. Phinney, 1842-48), 2:429; C. R. Fish, *Civil Service*, 91, 165.

Marcy, and Silas Wright, who were also the leading figures under Jackson in extending the spoils system nationally. That only one percent of N.Y. congressmen managed to win three consecutive renominations during 1838-56, cannot be unrelated to the influence of the Albany Regency in behalf of nomination rotation. And the fact that three-fourths of the withdrawals were freshmen, renders Kernell's assumption untenable, at least for the largest state, that the bulk of rotation was confined to sophomores.

Furthermore, the rates of withdrawal in columns a, b, and c of Table 3 indicate that rotation in New York was substantially stronger than in Pennsylvania or Ohio. A generous estimate for the effect of interparty competition in frightening congressmen into withdrawal,[66] would subtract

---

[66]According to Kernell's figures for five selected decades of the 19th century, the withdrawal rate averaged 44 percent in districts with party turnover (calculated from Kernell, p. 681, table 1). Formula A below assumes that in districts with party turnover, fully half the incumbents (50 percent) anticipated the worst and did not seek renomination for fear of defeat in the interparty competition. Kernell, however, disregards interparty competition of the 19th century as insignificant in promoting withdrawals (Kernell, 682).

Formula A

$$w' = \frac{X+Y}{2} + z$$

Where:
w = actual total withdrawals for state in question
w' = adjusted total withdrawals at hypothetical party turnover rate
x = number of districts in state with party turnover
y = additional number of districts with party turnover assuming some higher rate of party turnover

$$z = w - \left(\frac{X}{2}\right) \quad = \text{withdrawals not due to anticipated party turnover}$$

Under formula A, dividing w' by the size of the state's delegation in the expiring 10 Houses (N.Y., 358; Penn., 261; Ohio, 210) yields the adjusted withdrawal rate for a hypothetical party turnover rate. Applying New York's party

Table 3. *Percentage of Class to Withdraw, 1938-57*

	(a) all terms	(b) freshmen class	(c) soph. class	3+ termers	Kernell formula c - b	% districts with party turnover
New York	65	62	74	64	12	35
Pennsylvania	52	41	70	73	29	26
Ohio	40	28	60	47	32	21
Massachusetts	28	25	17	39	-8	11

Source: Appendix II

only five percent and six percent respectively from the margins by which Pennsylvania and Ohio trail New York in column a, and (assuming ambition was relatively equal in the three states) the remainder of New York's lead in the withdrawal rate is attributable to rotation. Yet according to Kernell's formula c minus b, Table 3) New York is by far the weakest of the three in supporting rotation. The relative strength of rotation in the three states, using the Kernell formula, is exactly the reverse of what columns a, b and c indicate.

It is clear, then, that the *modus operandi* whereby the withdrawal rate for freshmen is a "benchmark" against which to measure the effect of rotation in other classes is not valid for the antebellum period. In this light Kernell's formula is highly questionable for the postbellum rotation as well. Since freshmen were far more numerous than any other single class, and until 1876 usually constituted a majority of the House, the proportion of House careers ended by rotation must have been much larger indeed than

---

turnover rate to the other states adjusts the withdrawal rate upward to 57 percent for Pennsylvania and 46 percent for Ohio—still below the 65 percent rate for New York.

Kernell's estimate that is based exclusively on the set of congressmen who belonged to the sophomore class.[67]

In fairness to Professor Kernell, he does state that his effort is "an educated guess" about the relative effects of ambition, competition, and rotation. However, ranking the three factors according to their percentage effects on House turnover, is, for this writer, to stretch the empirical evidence beyond reasonable limits. The contributions of the three factors in terminating the House careers of the 19th century are, I believe, simply too causally interrelated, and their borders too indistinct, to be sorted out with any hope of factuality.

CONCLUSION

Rotation in office was a development of the American Revolution, with precedents dating back to several democracies of the ancient world. As typifies political revolutions, the fervor and altruism began to fade and political realities supplanted some of the original ideals. One casualty in the twelveth year of the new Republic was the law limiting incumbency in the Confederation Congress to three years.

The reader may find similarities in the fate of the "Self-Denying Ordinance" that the Constituent Assembly enacted early in the French Revolution, and also in the first of the revolutionary constitutions of France (1791) limiting membership in the Legislative Assembly to four years in six.[68] After the execution of Louis XVI, rotation in the legislative body was thrust aside by the radical convention but restored in the Thermidorean Reaction (constitution of 1795),[69] only to be minimized and finally abolished altogether by the Napoleonic constitutions of 1799 and 1804.[70]

---

[67]"In fact there is good reason to conclude that rotation accounts largely for the amazingly high turnover rates that characterized the House of Representatives throughout most of the nineteenth century. . . . Surely the practice of giving every county and every aspiring politician a turn had more than a casual bearing on this phenomenon." Laurence N. Powell, "Rejected Republican Incumbent," 235-36.

[68]Title III, Chapter I, Section Ill.6. Constitution of 1791.

[69]Constitution of the Year III, sections 54, 55, 137, 138.

[70]Constitution of the Year VIII, section 32; Constitution of the Year XII, section 78.

In America the new policy regarding tenure was neither complete nor violent. After ratification of the U.S. Constitution short tenure for Congress persisted on an extraconstitutional basis. But unlike the two-term tradition in the presidency, which became almost sacred with age,[71] the rotation of congressmen was tainted over several decades and discredited. From the age of Jackson onward spoilsmen came to the fore and distorted it into philosophy and policy quite different from the original.[72] Perhaps the geographic spread of the hundreds of nominating conventions, coupled with the lack of a constitutional system of nonpartisan rotation, made it inevitable that the extraconstitutional practice would sooner or later be politicized and diverted from service to the Republic as a whole.

For such reasons and others assessed in the text, the United States eventually embraced the antithesis of rotation, thereby culminating a conceptual revolution that was slow but sweeping. It was indeed a revolution, albeit long-term, because evolution moves more or less in one direction, whereas revolution breaks completely with a course or idea of the pact.

America's first revolt against old evaluations of tenure took place when the 13 United States instituted rotation in the Continental Congress. Parliament and monarchy in the Mother Country abhorred such Harringtonian aberrations.[73]

---

[71]In 1875, the House of Representatives passed by the extraordinary margin of 233 to 18 the following resolution:

Resolved, That, in the opinion of this House, the precedent established by Washington and other Presidents of the United States, in retiring from the presidential office after their second term, has become, by universal concurrence, a part of our republican system of government, and that any departure from this time honored custom would be unwise, unpatriotic, and fraught with peril to our free institutions.

Congressional Record, 44 Congress 1, 228. Half a century later an essentially identical resolution passed the Senate, 56 to 26. *CR* 70 Congress 1, 2842.

[72]Frederick N. Whitridge, "Rotation in Office," 282-84, 288-89.

[73]According to John Aubrey, a contemporary of James Harrington, all but eight or 10 members of Parliament in 1659 "hated" Harrington's plans for parliamentary rotation. John Aubrey, *Brief Lives Chiefly of Contemporaries. . . ,* ed. Andrew Clark, 2 vols. (Oxford: Clarendon Press, 1898), 1:291. See also, Edmund Burke, *Reflections on the Revolution in France* (Middlesex, England: Pelican Classics,

Today, the dominance of careerism in the House represents not only a radical departure from the past, but a counterrevolution. For the ascendancy of the idea of professional congressman first required a revolt, against a principle long prominent, that itself sprang from the American Revolution.

1968), 139.

APPENDIX

I. *Incumbent wins, losses and withdrawals. Original sources: Congressional Quarterly Weekly Report*, 1974, p. 1815, and November postelection issues since 1956. *Congressional Quarterly's Guide to U.S. Elections*, 1975, pp. 543-880. *Notable Names in American History*, 1973, pp. 70-266; *Biographical Directory of the American Congress*, 1774-1950 and 1774-1971 issues.

Membership lists for each House, as compiled in the last two works, are compared with electees to each subsequent House as given in *CQ's Guide to U.S. Elections*. Defeated incumbents are losers listed in the *Guide* who had any service at all in the expiring House. Winners similarly. Withdrawals are computed by adding the incumbent winners and losers, and subtracting the total from the number of seats in the expiring House. I delete secession from the withdrawal data for 1860-61.

II. *Break down by class: frosh vs. 2, 3, 4+ termers*. Sources: Same as Appendix I; also for 2, 3, 4+ termer defeats during the years 1838-65, *CQ's Guide to the Congress of the United States*, 1971, pp. 2a-175a. This work gives dates of service for all members of Congress in simple reference form. kind for the elections of 1906-76, each official *Congressional Directory*, 1st session, Congresses 60-95, breaks down the respective House membership into classes according to terms of previous service.

Chapter 5

Organizing by Party, Committees by Seniority, and Voting by Coalition

INTRODUCTION

A common complaint about the American Congress runs something like this: "The members never vote by straight party lines except on the matter of organization at the opening of a new Congress. After that all issues have to be worked out by complex bargaining processes, within committees dominated by seniority leaders, in floor action, and in adjusting differences between House and Senate. Party responsibility is dissipated, and the voters' ability to influence action by relying on party as a voting cue is undermined." Since the 1930s liberals in particular have felt that the "routine" party-line votes on organization should become the norm, and the Democratic congressional leaders have been remiss in not bringing pressure to bear upon those members—particularly southern Democrats—who are least likely to support a majority of their Democratic colleagues, or a Democratic president.

One line of research on voting patterns has sought to show that "party" is still a powerful predictor of congressional voting. Unfortunately, much of this research has not sought to separate out the independent effect of "party," holding other factors constant. But our purpose here is a different one. It is to explore some of the various ways in which American legislative bodies, state as well as federal, have gone about dealing with the problems of initial legislative organization as well as subsequent mustering of votes on substantive issues.

We shall assume that for Congress—and for most state legislatures—there are important factors making for diversity of response among legislators. Thus there are marked sectional differences, both national and within many states, rural-urban contrasts, city and state rivalries, as well as individual variations of policy outlook. The direct primary system of nomination has tended to take the control of nominations away from the party organization and to make each legislator more responsible for his own constituency backing. Moreover, the tendency of the minority party to atrophy under the direct primary probably increases the diversity of viewpoint represented within the majority party. Hence we shall be concerned with possible means within the legislative chamber for increasing party cohesion, given that there are tendencies to follow local or personal preferences.

We shall ask not only why "party" lines do not hold on most substantive issues, but why they do manage to hold on such important organizational questions as the election of a Speaker? It has not always been so. As recently as 1911, a Republican majority of the U.S. Senate was presided over by a Democratic president *pro tem*, because a band of seven Republican "Progressives" refused to vote for the regular Republican candidate. And in various state legislatures presiding officers may be elected by bipartisan voting blocs, a minority party plus some majority defectors, and a variety of other alignments other than the simple and seemingly automatic "party vote." Why, for example, did Virginia's powerful Congressman Howard D. Smith, longtime chairman of the influential Rules Committee, automatically vote for Sam Rayburn for Speaker—even when he and Rayburn were engaged in a fight to the finish over make-up of the committee?

We shall be concerned with three principal choice problems faced by virtually all state and federal legislative bodies in the United States. These are:

(1) Choice of a presiding officer, or other leaders.
(2) Choice of committee chairmen.
(3) Choice of committee members.

The way in which each of these is handled can have a substantial effect on what a legislative body does, or does not do. And the common criticism of recent congressional leaders has been that, as leaders (by virtue of choice process one, they should use their influence over precesses two and three so as to nudge recalcitrant colleagues into great party regularity in their voting on issues. Thus liberal critics of Democratic party leadership in Congress talk longingly of the use of "policy committees" or the "party caucus." But successive Democratic congressional leaders rival each other in the infrequency of resorting to such tactics. It would seem either that the leaders are missing a minor opportunity, or that the critics are missing some crucial aspect of the legislative game.

EVOLUTION OF HOUSE PRACTICE

Over the years the practice of the national House and Senate in regard to these three choice processes has varied widely. Indeed, it has varied extremely widely. But in general the solutions to each problem can be regarded as falling under the heading of being an automatic norm (such as "seniority" for committee chairmen), or as matters of discretion and hence resting upon some process of bargaining and coalition formation. With three functional problems to resolve—election of a leader, choice of committee chairmen, and choice of other committee members—and two alternative methods for each we are presented with an array of eight patterns for legislative organization. In fact, however, only four of these patterns seem to have been relied upon by the House or Senate. These four may be summarized, in order of increasing reliance on seniority, as follows (see Table 1).

It is useful to begin by considering the "normal" or simplest possible pattern for a legislative body, and then consider its possible evolution. Its first problem is to acquire some sort of presiding officer. If it can elect its own leader then the members will have leverage to bring to bear upon him such that the simplest solution to the appointment of committee members and chairmen is to have it done by the legislative leader. If the legislative body is to operate within a two-party system then one might expect each party to put up a candidate for leader. Whether committee appointments would be made for all members by the winner, or by each party for its own members is a more complex question.

The point we need to establish here is that the U.S. House, free to elect its own Speaker (even from outside its own membership, although this has never happened), initially moved towards this "simplest" pattern, which is Pattern I. It was a matter of decades before standing committees definitely

Table 1 . *Alternative Patterns for Handling Three Functional Problems of Organization in U.S. House and Senate*

Pattern	Choice of Comm. Chairman	Choice of Other Members	Choice of Party and/or Chamber Leader*
I	Coalitions	Coalitions	Coalitions
II	Seniority	Coalitions	Coalitions
III	Seniority	Seniority	Coalitions
IV	Seniority	Seniority	Seniority

Note: Vice president is official presiding officer of Senate.

replaced *ad hoc* ones, and after the Civil War before a stable two-party rivalship for the Speaker emerged. But from 1789 to after 1900 the House operated along some variation of Pattern I. That is to say, each of the three functional problems of organization were handled by coalition and bargaining processes, each of which had a strong effect on the other two. Changes in one would have major ramifications for the others.

The major choice points in the evolution of the national House are summarized in Figure 1. By the end of the very 1st Congress reliance on floor election for making up committees (then select ones, rather than standing ones) had yielded to appointment by the Speaker. Extensive executive domination developed in Washington's second term, with Hamilton taking the lead. This was less true under John Adams, but reasserted in a more subtle form under Jefferson. After Jefferson the House has been a pretty independent institution. But it did not become a two-party institution until the Jacksonian period, and this broke down in much of the 1850s.

The classic pattern of strong parties and centralized control by the Speaker developed after the Civil War. The choice of a Speaker, formerly wide open, was then restricted to competition between the party nominees. Incumbents were sometimes disposed, and Speakers frequently sought election to a Senate seat. Committee chairmen were appointed by the

Figure 1. Turnover of Committee Assignments and Organizational Structure in State Legislative Bodies of the United States

EXECUTIVE DOMINATION

One Party / Nonpartisan or Bipartisan — Single Authority Appoints Committees (nonseniority)

Committees Slated by: Comm. on Comm. — Single Legis. Auth. — Floor Election

TURNOVER:

Lower Chambers

High	Low	High	Low	High	Low
(nearly extinct) Alabama (at times)	(none)	(none)	(none)	(none)	CA (1930–1955) MN (de jure)

Upper Chambers

High	Low	High	Low	High	Low
Alabama (at times)	(none)	NE (unicameral)	MN (de jure)	(none)	(none)

NO EXECUTIVE DOMINATION

One Party — Committees Slated by: Floor Election — Comm. on Comm. — Single Legis. Auth.

TURNOVER:

Lower Chambers

High	Low	High	Low	High	Low
(none)	(none)	(none)	(none)	GA TN	MS VA LA

Upper Chambers

High	Low	High	Low	High	Low
(none)	VA SC	VT KS	(none)	TN	MS FL

Two Party — Committees Slated by: Comm. on Comm. — Single Legis. Auth. — Party Leaders — Floor Election

TURNOVER:

Lower Chambers

High	Low	High	Low	High	Low	High	Low
KY	AK	IN	NY RI NJ IL PA MN (de facto)	CN	(none)	(none)	(none)

Upper Chambers

High	Low	High	Low	High	Low	High	Low
KS	CA WI MI IL MN (de facto)	(none)	NY NJ PA	CN	(none)	OK CO	(none)

107

Speaker, with no presumption of seniority necessarily being followed. Since chairmanships were the prime trading materials by which a candidate might seek to win the Speakership, they were often given to members who were not those "next in line" on the committee, and frequently to members who had never served on the committee at all. Although a member who was "next in line" might be able to win the chairmanship of that committee, he had no guarantee of it (especially if it was an important committee), or of keeping it once he had obtained it. Thus committee chairmanships were highly unstable and subject to sharp change at every two-year period. Extent of the change would depend on whether there was a new Speaker, how popular a particular committee post was, and how many rival claimants were returned to the succeeding Congress.

Elsewhere I have described the processes for choosing committee chairmen and other members in the 19th century as follows:

> Every two years a member's committee assignment and even his continued service were at the mercy not just of the voters but of the majority party and the Speaker. A member of the minority might, and often was, removed from House membership by resort to the notorious "contested election" process. So-called contests could be claimed in almost any district, whether Maine or Georgia, and the candidate of the majority party in the House declared the winner. Up to 1907 of 382 "contests" only 3 were resolved in favor of the candidate of the minority party! Improvements in election administration and heightened public sensitivity to fraud have almost completely eliminated this threat to a member's career. And 19th century party nominations, made in the confusion of the delegate convention, were subject to little regulation.
>
> If a member was fortunate enough to be renamed by his party, reelected by the voters, and escape a partisan election contest he would return to a House where committee assignments and chairmanships were openly bartered for in the process of determining the party leadership (especially in the majority party, which would elect the Speaker). The support of freshmen members was courted as avidly, or more, than that of the relatively few veteran members. Thus after the Democrats captured the House in 1890 there was a sharp four-way fight for the Speakership among Roger Mills of Texas, who had been Ways and Means chairman in the 1887-88 Congress, C. F. Crisp of Georgia, William Springer of Illinois, and McMillin of Tennessee.

Fortunately we have a contemporary's account of how the 1891 Speakership contest referred to was resolved:

> On the first ballot in the caucus only a few votes separated Mills and Crisp, the leaders, and it was regarded as certain that one of them would be named. Then the dickering began among the managers of the candidates for high committee places, and the Crisp men out-generated the Mills' forces in that line of work. Judge Springer withdrew his name and voted for Crisp, and that settled it. Mr. Crisp was nominated, and Judge Springer secured the chairmanship of the Ways and Means Committee, and, as the floor leadership went with it as usual, he was satisfied with the outcome. The other Crisp managers got important committee assignments.[1]

The converse of this was that the few members who choose to remain in the House—and managed to do so—could in no way count on a stable, predictable career pattern. Not only was their very membership always in some doubt or danger, but also their committee posts were always subject to change with the coming of a new Congress. Consider the case of William Holman, a member of the Appropriations Committee and father of the famous "Holman rule" (permitting legislation in appropriations bills if this reduces expenditures):

> William Holman, one of the few really long-term 19th century members, specialized in appropriations during Randall's chairmanship. But instead of succeeding Randall on the committee, Holman was switched to Public Lands in the 50th and 51st Congresses, and in the 51st the Republicans named Sayers of Texas as top minority man on Appropriations. In the 52nd Congress Holman returned to Appropriations as chairman, but in the succeeding Congress again lost the post (to Sayers) and had to be satisfied with Indian Affairs.[2]

Writing in 1898, McConachie observed in regard to committee chairmanships in the House:

---

[1] O. O. Stealey, *Twenty Years in the Press Gallery* (New York: Publishers Printing Company, 1906), 106.

[2] H. Douglas Price, "The Congressional Career Then and Now," in *Congressional Behavior*, ed. Nelson W. Polsby (New York: Random House, 1971), 21.

The line of promotion has led from headship of some one of the others to headship of the finance committee. . . . Garfield advanced from the Military Affairs, 1867-1869, to the Banking and Currency, 1869-1871, then to the Appropriations, 1871-1875. . . . William S. Holman held three different chairmanships of two terms each. . . . The most striking record of all is that of William M. Springer, successively head of seven different committees.[3]

Influential House members cherished the right to ditch a middle-rank committee to make a play for one of the key committees, such as Appropriations or Ways and Means. The route to the chairmanship of one of these key committees was as likely to be via a switch from the chairmanship of a lesser committee as by long and faithful service on one of the latter.

Throughout the 19th century, then, the choice of House leaders was intimately linked with the naming of committee chairmen and members. Did this centralizing of authority in the hands of a leader permit him to enforce party unity? The answer seems to be generally no. James Young makes this quite clear for the case of Henry Clay in the early, preparty period. And in the later era, when party feeling did run strong, leaders still felt constrained to bargain away much of their presumed leverage. Thus major rival contenders for the Speakership usually were rewarded with chairmanship of Ways and Means (which for the Democrats generally included the floor leadership post) or Appropriations. Considerations of party policy could be invoked in regard to one or two committees or issues, but the base of support for the leader was too fragile and changing to permit rigorous enforcing of a party position. At least this was the case down to the election of 1896, from which time the movement toward the "modern" pattern of organization can be dated.

The disastrous Bryan campaign ended the close balance of party strength that had prevailed in many parts of the country. It also ushered in an era of straight Republican dominance over all three branches of government. The rapid turnover of House leadership and committee chairmen was sharply reduced, and the possibility of winning reelection as well as the advantages of doing so both soared. The election of 1900 was

---

[3]Lauros Grant McConachie, *Congressional Committees: A Study of the Origin and Development of Our National and Local Legislative Methods* (New York: Crowell, 1898), 159-60.

thus the first in U.S. history in which the percentage of freshmen House members was less than 30 percent (a figure was most recently exceeded in 1932) and also the first in which the average terms of service exceeded 3.0 (a figure below which it has never subsequently fallen). New all-time lows for freshmen members were set in 1904, 1908, and 1916; new all-time highs for average terms of service were set in 1904, 1906, and 1908.

After capturing the House in 1894 (after the panic of 1893) and extending their margin in the 1896 landslide, the Republicans seemed to have become a permanent majority party. And Joe Cannon, the autocratic speaker who, after 1902, sat at the peak of the centralized authority structure, seemed almost as permanent a fixture as Speaker. But Cannon presided over a party that was becoming very sharply divided. The lines between Progressives and Regulars in the GOP seem to have been as sharply drawn in the House around 1910 (and later in the Senate) as the split between southern and nonsouthern Democrats in the post-Roosevelt Democratic party.

Moreover, Cannon was the first Speaker in American history to be faced by a body that began to build up a substantial amount of seniority, both in terms of service in the chamber and on particular committees. This substantial "continuity" came to exist, even though the full-blown norm of seniority did not. Displacement of committee members traditionally had been the accompaniment of fights for a new Speaker, and in a body in which freshmen were one in five rather that two in five or even three in five. Since most chairmen and most members did not run sharply counter to Cannon there was no reason to question the reapportionment of most of them. This raised even more sharply the question of what was to be done in the case of those few, such as George Norris, who did not cooperate.

The outcome in 1910-1911 is well known and need not be reviewed at any length here. But it is important to note that Cannon faced a problem qualitatively different from that of any prior Speaker. And his actions were taken under circumstances (stability of majority party and of Speaker) that were also qualitatively different from the viewpoint of the members of the house. By 1910 the House had built up a system of substantial "continuity" in regard to membership of both the chamber and the committees. Here it is important to choose our words carefully. "Seniority" as such was not the issue—yet. How does a Speaker respond to a seemingly unique situation where he retains formal power to make or break any and all committee assignments, yet faces a body in which most of the members have developed stable expectations about a continuing "career" in the House and a pattern of continued service on their present or preferred committee assignments.

In 1910-1911 feelings of "party" were still strong, and a vigorous White House lead might have provided some sort of guideline. But Taft had disappointed the Progressives and lapsed into inactivity. Cannon was a partisan of the old school and stuck to the rough-and-tumble style of the 19th-century House. This was dangerous, and Norris and the Progressives managed to find a parliamentary loophole by which to attack. The Democrats had never embraced the full expanse of the strong Speakership practiced by Reed and Cannon but were willing to dismantle the office (which they expected to capture at the next election) entirely.

The assault could have run entirely to Cannon, but in fact it was directed more to the office of Speaker. The power to appoint committee members and chairmen was taken away and lodged in respective party committees. The Speaker was removed as chairman of the Rules Committee, and it was expanded in size. Other changes were made, and in general there was a reaction—to last from 1911 to about 1925 against the Speakership itself. The Democrats under Wilson looked to the majority leader, who served as chairman of Ways and Means, for leadership. And when the Republicans recaptured the House in 1918, they turned to a figurehead Speaker, who became the last Speaker to desert the House for election to the Senate, doubtless because the life of a figurehead is not all that interesting.

Thus two major changes had come upon the House, which upset the traditional pattern of open bargaining for leadership, chairmanships, and committee members. First, *de facto* continuity and increasing amounts of chamber seniority were present in the House to an absolutely unparalleled degree. Second, the appointment power was now collegial, and by party, rather than centralized (from 1902 to 1910 Cannon had informally delegated minority appointments to the minority leader—thus helping to stabilize that role) and overall members. The pressures of more members with prior service and desiring to carve out stable long-run careers in the House vastly increased. At the same time the incentive and power to manipulate appointments, in order to win central leadership or in the name of "party," was gone. Could decentralized appointment influence, held by large committees in each party, resist the pressures toward converting *de facto* "continuity" into a *de jure* system of absolute committee seniority?

We know that the answer is no, but the causal situation in regard to the House is confused by the presence of two variables (decentralization of appointing authority, as well as increased presence of members with more prior service and greater desire for long-term career). Which was the more important? Could a more flexible Speaker than Cannon have survived the increased desire for stable House careers and continued to have maintained some discretion of appointment even in a system of "substantial continuity?"

The factors relating to the continued existence of a fluid pattern based on coalition formation and the emergence of the new pattern (type II) of automatic seniority for committee chairmen are summarized in Table 1, Chapter 2. And the evolutionary path traced by the House as it moved through successive decisive choices has been summarized in Figure 1. The evidence of the House experience would suggest that coalitions and bargaining prevailed prior to around 1900, but that the norm of seniority was well-nigh irresistible by 1919. It is obvious that "continuity" built up, both in the chamber and on committees, in the period 1900-1910. And the "syndication" of the Speakership into plural bodies, separately organized for each party. These committees on committees—the Democrats relying on their members on Ways and Means but the Republican using a more complex special committee—proved much more vulnerable to claims of prior service and alleged "seniority" rights. But does the development of low turnover and shift to collegial appointments by party necessarily open the door to seniority? If so, which of these two conditions is the more important factor? From the single case of the House we can draw no conclusion, but similar situations had previously occurred in the case of the national Senate—where low turnover and collegial appointment both were the pattern even before the Civil War. And they have occurred in many of our state legislative chambers more recently. Hence we shall expand our analysis—in brief form—to compare the situation and its evolution in these other legislative bodies. The national House suggests a guiding hypothesis; the experience of a hundred other legislative bodies help to shed additional light on it.

STATE LEGISLATIVE PATTERNS

The House and Senate patterns are consistent and highly suggestive of trends that should be clearly observable among the 99 state legislative bodies. To complete our canvas we shall briefly summarize the situation for state legislatures. With longer sessions, higher pay more staff assistance, they are becoming much more similar to the modern, post-1900, Congress. But in many states they are still characterized by high membership turnover. We shall be concerned to sort out the patterns of leadership selection, committee appointment procedures, and reliance on seniority.

Full information on the practices of the state legislatures is not readily available for the current period, much less for the past. But detailed information is available over time for certain legislatures, and some basic items of information are readily on hand for all legislative bodies of the states. Thus we shall canvass the materials that are generally available.

Even if full data were available it would not necessarily represent 99 independent tests of the hypotheses suggested by our analysis of the national legislative chambers. The chief difficulty—well known to anthropologists under the name of "Galton's problem"—is that certain practices are likely to have been adopted by imitation or diffusion rather than because of the casual impact of certain characteristics of the units considered. This is a problem of great importance for systematic study of cities or state as well as for cross-national research. It would remain an important alternative hypothesis, even if complete data on all states were available.

We shall begin with the lower houses, where variation is less. The early national pattern of extensive executive dominance lived on well into the twentieth century at the state level, but is now almost extinct. As of 1949, Belle Zeller classed five state legislatures as "executive-dominated," but by the mid 1960s this class seems to have shrunk to only Alabama. The national House's next pattern of nonpartisan operation in the age of Clay was represented by the California house as late as the mid-1950s but now is extinct except for the unicameral nonpartisan Nebraska chamber. Flexible committee appointments by a single authority, in two-party context with turnover, was true of the national House from 1830 to the 1850s, and was standard pattern from Reconstruction to around 1900. After results of 1896 turnover dropped, and after 1902 the minority usually could make its own appointments through its leader (the modern Conn. Pattern). As pointed out previously, up to 1950 no state lower chamber had moved to use of committees on committees, and up to now this exits formally in only two of 50 states. Thus almost all state lower houses still operate in situations more comparable to the pre-1910 national House, having centralized appointment without rigid seniority. A significant number still have such high membership turnover as to resemble even the pre-1896 national House, though a number of the large industrial states of the northeast have low turnover that makes them more comparable to the House of the decade 1900-1910.

It may be useful to note first some state chambers that display patterns long since extinct at the national level. Thus in regard to executive dominance the Alabama and Tennessee legislatures can usefully be compared to Congress in the days of Washington, Jefferson, or perhaps Jackson. But this is a rare pattern, and one likely to be disrupted by the development of a more effective party politics.

Some other states operate along bipartisan or nonpartisan lines. Thus the California legislature, from 1920 to the mid-1950s, operated on cross-party lines. Speakers were elected by cross-party factions (though Republicans were dominant), and members of both parties were rewarded with committee chairmanships. William Buchanan's excellent book on legislative partisanship is a perceptive account of the change from this to a more customary party-oriented system (although this change is still not complete). The "nonpartisanship" of Minnesota is largely nominal, though the absence of party labels from the ballot has some real effects. Nebraska's one-house nonpartisan legislature may be a close replica of the national scene in the "era of good feelings" and of absence of clear party ties.

There is, however, one pattern for state legislative organization that does not seem to have occurred at the national level in any era. This is *rotation* of key chairmanships and the leadership, such as is done in New Jersey and North Carolina. This procedure would seem useful for a one-party state as a means of avoiding the centralization of power around a Speaker without the restraints of a party system (functionally comparable to the ban on gubernatorial reelection). In a two-party context it is harder to understand, but it may reflect a sharing of oligarchical control compatible with a relatively small chamber (as both New Jersey chambers are). At the turn of the century the U.S. Senate was dominated by an elderly oligarchy, which shared floor leadership but did not rotate committee posts. Given the Senate's early and strong commitment to committee seniority, rotation could hardly develop in that regard.

In regard to the appointment of committees and chairmen the situation in state lower Houses is relatively simple. In 45 of the 49 lower chambers the Speaker does so with no formal restrictions. In Connecticut, a state with exceptionally strong party organizations, the minority appointments are made by the minority leader (this is true for both House and Senate, the state being one of three that relies largely on joint committees). And in New Mexico the Speaker's preferences are supplemented by an advisory committee. In only two of the 49 states is the national pattern followed and appointments made by a collegial group. The two deviations are Alaska, which seems to have followed the national pattern by imitation, and Kentucky, which has moved to committee in committees within the last decade.

In regard to seniority, our dependent variable, Arkansas is the only state known to follow a strict seniority rule. Although Alaska uses committees, strict seniority is not followed. Thus it would appear that for as many as 46 of the 49 lower chambers committee appointments are made by the speaker, and made on a flexible basis. There are obvious differences in the degree of membership turnover and of committee continuity, but the absolute "seniority norm" is reported nowhere outside Arkansas.

So long as state Speakers can avoid getting themselves into the sort of corner that Joseph Cannon did, they should be able to maintain some discretion. Even in states with very great membership stability—equaling or even exceeding that of the national House—Speakers have maintained discretion. This is particularly so in cases where they can depend on the power and legitimacy of their party's governor or the state party organization.

To test whether a Speaker can retain some discretionary power over chairmen and appointments even in a body with low turnover we have only to find a state legislature corresponding to these characteristics. As Figure 1 indicates, New York seems to have been the pioneer in regard to high continuity and low turnover of its lower house—for 1925-35 it had a lower percentage of freshmen members than did the national House. Has this marked and unusual degree of continuity undermined the Speaker's appointment power, or does he still retain some significant discretion?

Fortunately a detailed study of the New York legislature has recently been completed by Professor Stuart Witt. He reports that Speakers (almost always Republican) have served very lengthy periods, major committee chairmen have also served lengthy periods, and general turnover of members has been very low. The legislature operates in a highly professionalized state government and alongside a governor with very extensive power. But a legislative career is valued, especially outside New

York City. Under Republican organization the New York Speakers have retained considerable leverage. But it is to be exercised on behalf of party programs, as defined by the governor (if Republican), and is made effective by the power of the governor to influence local party organization.

The 1964 Goldwater disaster brought in a Democratic majority, and a contest for the Speakership. Eventually, the Republicans broke the deadlock by throwing their votes behind one of the two Democratic rivals. Despite the great emphasis on continuity in New York the successful Democratic candidate for Speaker was still able to see that his Democratic supporters were disproportionately rewarded (there being no crossing of lines in chairmanships):

> It should also be noted that while Travia in the leadership fight received the votes of only 40 percent of his party, 67 percent of the eighteen most important committees (measured in terms of 1966 workload) were given to his supporters, and 67 percent of the eighteen least important committees went to Steingut supporters.[4]

The victorious candidate took for himself, as is usual in New York, and was usual in the pre-1910 House, the chairmanship of the key Rules Committee. The other four most important committees, as measured by number of bills killed or reported, received chairmen as follows:

Ways and Means	Satriale	16 years service
Codes	Corso	16 years service
Judiciary	Turshen	28 years service
Labor & Industry	Rossetti	12 years service

The extent to which the centralized authority of the pre-1910 House lives on in many current state legislative chambers (especially lower houses) can be seen from the experience of states other than New York. Thus Duane Lockard, writing in 1958, describes the lower house of the Rhode Island legislature thusly:

> The legislative leaders in both Houses are respected, feared, and followed by the membership. In the House, the Speaker, Harry F. Curvin

---

[4]We have been unable to find the source of this quote (editor).

of Pawtucket, is as formidable a figure as was the awesome Speaker Cannon in the early years of this century in Congress. Curvin appoints committees and designates their chairmen and with the help of a few others he controls their actions. While presiding, Curvin has been known to gavel the House into adjournment rather than to allow a roll call that has been demanded. . . . Curvin has been in the House since 1931 and has been Speaker since 1941. . . .

The second most powerful figure in the House is the majority leader, James H. Kiernan. Although he was born in 1884, he remains spry and nimble-witted. An able speaker and master of invective when the occasion calls for it—as the occasion often seems to do—Kiernan has been in the House since 1915. . . . Without but one interruption he has been chairman of the powerful Judiciary Committee since 1935. In cooperation with Speaker Curvin, Kiernan controls virtually all the time of the House.[5]

Thus Rhode Island, like New York, has high membership stability, but has maintained a centralized appointment system. As with New York this would seem to have been buttressed by the role of extralegislative organization (thus the Mr. Kiernan that Lockard describes is the legislative leader of the Providence city Democratic machine, and his control of the Judiciary Committee is important for state judicial appointments).

Around the turn of the century George Haynes compiled extensive information on the characteristics of legislators in all of the states for which he could obtain data. Keeping in mind that the modern proportion of national House and Senate members with prior experience in their own chamber (a distinction that Haynes did not make) runs around 85 percent, it is striking that in 1900 only one of 27 lower state houses exceeded the 60 percent mark (Rhode Island was top with 62.5). But there were six of 29 state Senates above the 80 percent mark. Incidentally, New England tended to have among the highest figures for state Senates (all six were over 70 percent), but among the lowest for lower houses.

Haynes suggests that under town representation there was much rotation of office among individuals, a practice obviously running counter to the development of an effective professionalized legislature. Career data on all

---

[5]Duane Lockard, *New England State Politics* (Princeton: Princeton University Press, 1950), 217-18.

Massachusetts Speakers tend to bear out that nonprofessionalized nature of that body throughout most of the 19th century, in which Speakers were sometime under 30 years of age and frequently moved on to other offices (one who was a minister subsequently became chaplain of the state Senate). Haynes' data on members with prior legislative experience can be summarized as follows:

Number of State Chambers with Indicated Percentage of Members with Some Previous Legislative Experience (in either Chamber)

	0-19	20-39	40-59	60-79	80 and over
29 State Senates:	3	6	6	8	6
27 State Houses:	9	10	7	1	0

Belle Zeller's 1950 study of state legislatures presents some amazing contrasts in degree of legislative turnover. Thus in the following table (for lower House), the first figure represents the number of freshmen and the second figure the number of members with five terms or more:

Very Low Turnover States (ratio 4/1 or more)		High Turnover States (ratio 1/2 or less)	
Alabama	61/0	Illinois	31/72
Arizona	32/8	Louisiana	6/19
Arkansas	47/10	Mississippi	2/22
Colorado	38/7	New Jersey	4/25
Connecticut	121/23	New York	2/93
Delaware	25/0	Rhode Island	15/45
Georgia	101/20		
Indiana	64/14		
Kansas	60/6		
Kentucky	50/3		

High Turnover States (ratio 4/1 or more)		Low turnover States (ratio less than 5/4 but above 1/2)	
Maine	76/7	California	21/18
Maryland	67/2	Massachusetts	67/60
Nevada	20/5	Michigan	20/17
New Mexico	27/3	Minnesota	33/39
Ohio	44/11	Virginia	25/24
Oklahoma	60/6	West Virginia	16/16
Tennessee	58/3	Wisconsin	28/25
Utah	30/6		
Vermont	131/12		
(all others between 4/1 and 5/4)			

Obviously in terms of experience the Alabama legislature is a vastly different sort of institution than say, New York. As of 1950 Alabama had first-term chairmen for all 14 House Committees, and for 23 of 30 separate committees—in New York 20 of 36 House Chairmen had served 10 or more sessions, and the remaining 16 had all served from five to nine sessions.

The general level of turnover is suggested by Charles Hyneman's important study of 10 states for the period 1925-1935, in which the overall average of service was as follows:

	Sessions of Service				
	1st	2nd	3rd	4th	5th or more
Average of 10 lower houses	39.6	23.8	12.9	7.8	15.8
Average of 10 Senates	20.3	19.3	14.3	11.9	44.2

Thus lower chamber members in their first or second term were more than twice as common as were Senate members, whereas senators with five or more terms were three times as common as such experienced house members.

When compared with the distribution of freshmen in the 50 elections to the 19th-century national House, the patterns of nine of the 10 lower state chambers clearly fall into the same situation of high turnover. The most striking exception is New York, followed by Illinois. The latter state has had one of the highest levels of pay for state legislators, and the system of cumulative voting has also insulated them to a large degree from general election defeat. But the pattern of New York, which seems to have followed the "professionalization" of the national House at almost the same time, has already been noted.

Over time there has been a considerable drop in legislative turnover at the state level, especially in lower houses. Our general view of the legislative process would suggest that this is a particularly crucial change, and valuable indicator. Unfortunately, there are only limited data available on turnover time. We do know that for the sessions studied by Wahlke, Eulau *et al.* the percentage of freshmen members in the California and New Jersey lower houses was in both cases less than half that found by Hyneman for those states a quarter century earlier (freshmen in California dropped from 40.7 to 17 percent, and in New Jersey from 37.2 to 15 percent). David Derge has noted a somewhat weaker trend to reelection in Indiana, but Indiana is exceptional in the very large proportion of districts that may go to either party.

Thus Speakers in states such as New York or Rhode Island are faced by members with long tenure, little turnover, and in a strong partisan setting. These are the conditions that Cannon faced nationally. But the New York Speakers have preserved their position, both to violate seniority in naming chairmen on some occasions and to control the Rules Committee. They have been able to do this it would seem, by pursuing their course with more caution than did Cannon. And, equally important, by fortifying their own role with the legitimacy of "party" and often with open backing of the governor (if of the same party) or outside party organization. Cannon did not legitimize his personal stand with the cloak of "party," nor did he enjoy the support of the chief executive. Indeed, after the celebrated 1910-1911 revolt Cannon was defeated for reelection in his own home constituency (though he subsequently was returned for another four terms, after which he retired).

For Cannon to so dominate his party purely on the basis of his own idiosyncratic preferences accorded with no known theory of representation or majority rule. Indeed, as early as 1898 McConachie noted that the power of the Speaker had become so great that it might be wise to have the Speaker chosen by a national election. This would be awkward, but it does suggest the importance of legitimizing the role, or of reducing the autocratic influence of the holder of it. Most state legislatures have moved in the former direction, via executive leadership in legislation if not outright domination or by emphasizing the duties of the Speaker as responsible party leader. But a few one-party states—one thinks of Mississippi or South Carolina—still give great leeway to their Speakers without such restraint.

Possibilities for change away from the centralized, flexible pattern are much greater in regard to state Senate. In these bodies the turnover is generally less, with a smaller membership and usually longer terms. And, as with the national Senate, there is the problem of the role of lieutenant governor, in states where that office exists. Just as the federal Senate revolted against vice-presidential leadership in the matter, so a majority of states have moved away from such a procedure. In only 12 of the 50 upper chambers (counting Nebraska) is appointment of committees by the lieutenant governor acting in his own capacity of president of the Senate. In another 14 the Senate's own president, the appointing authority, and in an additional seven the power is vested explicitly in the president *pro tem*, so as to bypass the lieutenant governor. This pattern includes the politically important states of New York, Ohio, and Pennsylvania. There are 12 states, all but one of them west of the Great Lakes and none from the South, that follow the national pattern and rely on committees. These include Wisconsin, Michigan, Minnesota, Illinois, and California, as well as Vermont (the sole eastern example) and Alaska. This leaves four states (Colorado, Virginia, Oklahoma, and South Carolina) that manage to operate on the oldest pattern of all, floor election.

Although the appointing authority for committees in each state is readily available, our information on turnover of membership and seniority is less complete than for state houses. Thus Haynes' 1900 data shows senators with any prior legislative experience, presumably including freshmen senators with prior house experience. And Belle Zeller's data show service by number of legislative sessions, which may be annual or biennial, and mix senators serving two- and four-year terms.

But comments that give a very high degree of importance to seniority practices in state Senates are frequent. Thus the survey by *Roll Call* quotes the president *pro tem* of the California Senate, a small body with very low turnover as saying that it uses "mainly seniority" which "eliminates the problem of evaluation of their abilities to a great extent." It also eliminates the flexibility of open coalition and bargaining, as well as the possibility of extensive executive involvement. Kansas, which has a high rate of turnover (due to rotation practices), also has a committee on committee procedure, and in that state "seniority is given considerable weight." Indeed, Kansas turnover is so high that any prior service may be both rare and valued.

Contrast these comments with the following statement from the Senate president of Maryland, a state where seniority is not the rule and executive involvement is frequent:

> After twenty years in the legislature, I am still trying to decide whether a seniority system would be an improvement. Sometimes I think the achievement of legislative independence would be worth the price.

The parallels between the evolution of national practice in regard to committees and chairmen and the varieties of state Senate practices is obvious. One need only note that the ancient Senate practice of electing committees and chairmen still seems to hang on in four state Senates, and that a large block of state Senates, including those of several large states, have adopted the subsequent Senate pattern of relying on party committees on committees. But a majority of state Senates have continued to permit appointment of committees by a single presiding officer, more often the Senate's own internal president or president *pro tem*, but in some cases the vice president acting as Senate president.

In general state Senates have fewer members, longer terms, and larger districts than do the house chambers. As a result most state Senates have markedly lower turnover rates—on the order of 50 percent lower—than do the lower houses. But there are exceptions. Some lower houses have large numbers of multiple-member districts, which may be as large as Senate districts. And a few Senates have multicounty districts where rotation of office is the practice. This has long been the practice in Kansas, for example. And in that state turnover in the Senate is exceptionally high—averaging 77.3 percent from 1901-1957—and higher than that for the lower house (where the average was 54.8 percent for same period).

Figure 1 presents a topology of state-level practices, for both lower and upper houses. Lack of data precludes entering every state chamber, but examples are shown where the necessary data are available. The pattern for state houses is actually simpler than it appears, since most of the cases fall into two or three of the possible categories. Several long-run trends are shifting the balance of cases among categories. Bipartisan or nonpartisan systems are now gone, except for Nebraska's unicameral chamber (Minnesota is nonpartisan in a formal sense only, there being partisan-type organizations in the legislature). More states are becoming two-party, so the list of one-party contexts is shrinking. And there is a marked shift of states from high turnover to low turnover, especially in regard to lower chambers. Finally, the use of committee on committees is a growing and important pattern for state Senates, and now has a small beachhead among lower houses also.

Strong tendencies are present at the state level to increase the "continuity" of committee appointments. In the absence of counterforces to maintain some flexibility this high continuity might well be expanded into a rigid "seniority" system, as occurred at the level of the national House between 1910 and the 1920s. The added legitimacy of the following national practices can also be considered as a possible factor. But for many states there are still counter-tendencies including the awareness of Speakers that their power is not absolute. And there is also the possibility of relying on the executive or on extralegislative party organization for support in maintaining a flexible, party-oriented pattern.

CONCLUSION

It is ironic to note that the firming up of seniority in the national House began under Woodrow Wilson, and the last real chance to challenge it came under Franklin Roosevelt. The Wilsonian pattern of reliance on party caucus and the leading role of Ways and Means was a temporary expedient, not a permanent solution. It was not strong enough to avoid the reestablishment of the Speaker as dominant over the floor leader, or the powerful demands for absolute "seniority." In 1933 it might have been possible for Roosevelt to use his immense popularity and the spirit of crisis to go back to some Wilsonian pattern, or at least to try and avoid giving the final stamp of approval to seniority, which had been followed in virtually every Democratic promotion of the 1920s and in all but a small handful of the Republican ones (and most of these exceptions involved Progressives who had broken with their party, either in support of LaFollete for president in 1924 or in refusing to vote for the regular party candidate for Speaker). But Roosevelt saw no immediate need to do so. For most of his first term he got about as much cooperation from southern committee chairmen as from the few nonsoutherners, so he seemed to have little to gain. But after 1937 the importance of southern strength in the seniority rankings—which is only now being challenged by central city Democrats from the North—became apparent.

The range within which bargains can be made and the extent to which such coalitions can be involved in committees on floor votes is thus much *more* extensive in the states than in the national House. Existence of effective party organization, in control of the nomination process, is also more common in at least several states than in regard to the national House (where it is hardly known at all except for Cook County Democrats).

We conclude that the reluctance of national congressional leaders to seek to compel greater voting support from members by threatening to upset long established patterns of committee appointment and seniority is reasonable. Cannon failed in such an effort—crudely undertaken, to be sure—even when he had the added formal powers that modern Speakers do not have. At the national level the meaning of "party" has shriveled, and the strength of extralegislative party organization declined, both of which undercut possible sources of support for congressional leaders. What has been substituted at the national level, and increasingly in the states, is vigorous executive leadership in regard to an official "administration" legislative program and executive plays a large role, but one in which legislative leaders are limited to marginal or incremental functions.

II. In the Literature: Two Critical Looks

Chapter 6

History of Ethics in Congress:
Three Perspectives

INTRODUCTION

Mentioning to colleagues that I was doing a paper on the topic of ethics and the history of Congress typically draws the jibe: "That will be a short paper." Actually, the subject is extremely broad. Whole books have been written on the question of seating members-elect and grounds for explusion: *Rebellion, Racism, and Representation* by P. A. Dionisopoulos (1970) is a good summary from the 1790s through the Adam Clayton Powell case. But there are broader questions that are equally relevant and seldom researched. And past disputes, even ones settled by resort to violence, duels in particular, can provide helpful perspective on the obstacles to change. It may be as useful to consider the pre-Civil War problem of dueling, which in good Aristotelian fashion has a beginning, a middle, and an end, as to complain about PACs, where we have only a beginning.

First, we should take due note of the legal position of Congress and its members in the federal Constitution and of the importance of British parliamentary precedents (as understood, or perhaps misunderstood, in 1787). The Constitution followed British practice in proclaiming the power of each chamber to judge the qualifications of its members. But this did

---

This chapter was originally prepared for delivery at the 1983 annual meeting of the American Political Science Association.

little more than to deny that the jurisdiction would go to some other branch of government (the king in the British case).

On most of the more common ethical issues such as "conflict of interest" or conduct of elections British practice provided no help at all. Rather, it provided an undesirable pattern of institutionalized specialized interests (land in the House of Lords and land plus other interests in the Commons). The violence and fraud common in British contested elections (see Hogarth's splendid four paintings of a parliamentary contest) would be regarded as reprehensible in most parts of the Third World today, if not perhaps in Chile or the Philippines. Obvious sources for the unattractiveness of British practice are Sir Lewis Namier's classic *The Structure of Politics at the Accession of George III* (on which interests controlled which seats), and H. J. Hanham's *Elections and Party Management* (on the reality of electoral management in the 19th century). In short, the British were a great source for parliamentary procedure—Jefferson's manual and the early rules of House and Senate were much indebted—but British parliamentary institutions and norms were not a very useful source for dealing with conflict of interest, contested elections, control of electoral fraud, or most other practical problems of legislative ethics.

In this paper I seek to explore three different analytic approaches to the history of ethics in Congress, other than the basic but well-trod legal approach. Anyone desiring a list of all known censures, reprimands, or expulsions can consult the standard publications of *Congressional Quarterly*, or write their member and ask him or her to pester some clerk at the Congressional Research Service.

My initial intent was to look in some detail at three well-documented "cases" that raise basic issues of congressional ethics in different historical periods (e.g., pre-Civil War, post-Civil War, and 20th century). But as I sought to narrow the choice of cases down I became more and more intrigued by the alternative analytic lenses that can used for viewing the material. Several excellent documented cases happen to be ready at hand in the five-volume compilation of landmark congressional investigations edited by Arthur Schlesinger, Jr., and Roger Bruns. To a degree, incomplete at this point, I have sought to develop each perspective in the context of a well-known historical "case," where extensive documentation is readily available.

The three perspectives that have intrigued me are: (1) ethical conflict resulting from differing political subcultures, each with its own distinctive ethical perspective; (2) Neustadt-style comparative case analysis; (3) relevance of modern "collective choice" theory to explaining individual member behavior in a case involving ethical problems. I am, of course, under no illusions that any of these, and especially the last, are likely to displace John F. Kennedy's *Profiles in Courage* in either popularity or sales.

PART I: POLITICAL CULTURE AND ETHICAL CONFLICT

McDuffie wanted pistols, but Metcalfe selected rifles. A hopeless impasse resulted. McDuffie's second, James Hamilton, Jr., claimed that McDuffie's crippled arm—a casualty of a previous duel—left him unable to handle a rifle. Metcalfe's agent replied that the gentleman challenged had the right to select the weapons. Besides, McDuffie's transcendent skill with pistols in the duello was well-known. After both contestants refused broad swords, Metcalfe's assistant suggested an alternative. Suppose two posts were erected to hold the rifles. The combatants would then merely march to their respective weapons, already secured in position, and fire at the proper time. McDuffie would not be forced to use his inferior limb at all. McDuffie wanted no part in this scheme, so the duel was called off.

Roger A. Bruns[1]

Much of what subsequent generations regard as simple ethical blindness may be better understood, though not necessarily approved, in terms of differing political cultures. Former House Rules Committee chairman Richard Bolling, surely one of the most astute as well as most highly principled members of Congress, has often spoken of the very sharp differences in perspective between members coming from areas of "court-house ring" southern politics or big-city "machine" politics as contrasted to those raised in more "public-regarding" or straight-laced environments.

Difficult questions of ethics can rise from the conflict of differing political cultures. But they also develop in situations of deviance from a generally accepted norm, something usefully emphasized by Kai Erikson's

---

[1]Arthur M. Schlesinger, Jr., and Roger Bruns, *Congress Investigates: A Documented History, 1792-1974* (New York: Chelsea Publications, 1975), I, 497.

brilliant reconstruction of the Salem witch trials in his book *Wayward Puritans.*

How did differing political cultures and codes of ethics effect Congress in the pre-Civil War period? If we set aside the major substantive issues, the processes of political life in the "Washington community" seem to have been profoundly influenced by the considerable conflict between "southern honor" and the North's increasing commitment to either the demands of conscience or of self-interest (the last two nicely illustrated by the two wings of the Whig Party in some northern states). The roots and implications of the South's special orientation are brilliantly developed (over close to 600 pages) in Bertram Wyatt-Brown's recent book on *Southern Honor: Ethics & Behavior in the Old South* (1982).

The quote at the beginning of this section makes the point. When charges were brought that John C. Calhoun was secretly involved in a contract to supply stones for a fort to protect the entrance to Chesapeake Bay (at Rip-Rap shoals)—a site not yet suggested for the MX system—his defense was undertaken by South Carolina's leading duelist. The southern code of honor, which had once held sway as far north as the Hudson River, where Burr and Hamilton fought (and Hamilton died), raises both the problem of a subculture at odds with the law (dueling was outlawed in the District of Columbia, and an increasing number of states) and the broader emerging culture, and of situations of conflict between individuals representing different subcultures. For the latter there are three possible patterns:

(1) Two members might both subscribe to the code of honor, and follow it, in violation of the law and the broader code of ethics.

(2) Two members might both *not* accept the code and limit their dispute to more conventional means.

(3) However, conflict often developed between a member who subscribed to the code and another member who did not.

(a) For the member who subscribed to the code there were then acceptable alternatives, such as caning. This required superior size and strength or the advantage of surprise (Senator Charles Sumner was of NFL size but had very poor eyesight and was taken unaware at his desk which served to trap his ample frame after the first blow).

(b) Members not subscribing to the code were often unaware of their precarious position.

Several levels of ethical conflict involving cultural differences are illustrated by the Herman J. Viola case in the Schlesinger-Bruns series, "Indian Rations and Sam Houston's Trial, 1832." The case arose in the course of ex-Congressman Sam Houston's efforts to obtain a highly profitable contract to provide rations for something over a year for roughly 80,000 eastern Indians during their "relocation" west of the Mississippi River (a prime goal of Jackson's first administration). Here, of course, we have a tragic substantive issue bordering on genocide. But for the purpose at hand I want to look at the more narrow questions of bribery and improper influence in efforts to obtain the huge contract (which would run to several millions of dollars in 1832 terms), resort to physical violence against a member of the House, and the institution's response.

Houston was a favorite of President Jackson, who was himself the survivor of more than one duel (though usually of the less elegant frontier variety). Jackson apparently wanted the contract to go to Houston. But presidential power is, as always, limited, and there was need for advertising for bids. If ample time was allowed, communications still being very slow (Alan R. Pred's *Urban Growth and the Circulation of Information*, page 177 has isotherms for rates of travel as of 1830), the contract would doubtless go to a low-cost western supplier. A shorter time would operate to ensure an eastern supplier. Unfortunately, nothing (linear programming had not been developed) would operate to ensure an adequate supplier. At any rate, there were bids lower than Houston's, and much delay and haggling ensued. It would be more profitable, in fact, for various relatively low bidders to join in a partnership at a higher bid. Removal was delayed, and the ads for bids finally withdrawn. The job of feeding the Indians went to the army, which itself had to contract for provisions.

Then in 1832 Ohio Congressman William Stanberry launched a partisan blast at Jackson in which he touched on the question of a fraudulent attempt to give the contract to Houston. Stanberry's floor remarks were published. Houston, who had returned to Washington, issued a formal challenge to Stanberry, who refused to acknowledge it (thus we are in pattern (3) above, with Houston moving to the (3a) subroutine). James K. Polk, who held Houston's old House seat, and others managed to restrain him from an assault on Stanberry *within* the Capitol itself—please note that this represents progress in the evolutionary development of congressional ethics.

Stanberry hoped to avoid Houston (like McDuffie he had only one functioning arm), but eventually their paths crossed. When Houston approached and inquired if he were Stanberry the latter replied in the affirmative and made a short bow. Houston shattered the hickory cane (which he had cut back at the Hermitage estate of Jackson's in Tennessee) on Stanberry's head and knocked him down. Stanberry drew a gun, but it misfired, and Houston continued his assault.

Stanberry survived with only minor physical damage but demanded that the House itself arrest Houston (an ex-member) and bring him to trial before that body. That proved to be a major tactical error, as Houston gloried in his role. It took over a month to get a narrow margin for a nominal reprimand. Subsequent historians have invented an overly precise party breakdown for this Congress (22nd) of 141 Democrats, 58 National Republicans, and 14 others. Jackson and Houston, if not God, were clearly on the side of the larger battalions. Jackson openly praised Houston's action, criticized the reprimand, and eventually remitted a court-imposed $500 fine.

The case did stake a useful new precedent, that the House could (at least in theory) protect a member from assault beyond the grounds of the Capitol. Of course, the Sumner assault shows backsliding in the heat of the 1850s slavery dispute. Stanberry was denied renomination in Ohio. He lived to see the overthrow of the southern code by the North's victory in the Civil War and died in January 1873, on the very day that Washington newspapers reported the testimony of Congressman Oakes Ames in the Credit Mobiliér scandal. If one vexing problem was largely solved, a major new one was attracting attention.

Before turning to the post-Civil War period we should note that interest in different political cultures with different ethical orientations is still very much with us. Almost 20 years ago Daniel Elazar's *American Federalism: A View from the States* sought to map the entire country in terms of three contrasting political orientations. For Elazar the three dominant orientations are spelled out in pages 86-94:

(1) "The individualistic political culture emphasizes the conception of the democratic order as a marketplace. In its view, a government is instituted for strictly utilitarian reason. . . . Since the individualistic political culture emphasizes the centrality of private concerns, it places a premium on limiting community intervention. . . .

" . . . In such a system, an individual can succeed politically, not by dealing with issues in some exceptional way or by accepting some concept of good government and then striving to implement it, but by maintaining his place in the system of mutual obligations.

(2) "The moralistic political culture emphasizes the commonwealth conception as the basis for democratic government. Politics . . . is considered one of the great activities of man in his search for the good society—a struggle for power, it is true, but also an effort to exercise power for the betterment of the commonwealth.

"Consequently, there is a general insistence that government service is public service, which places moral obligations upon those who participate in government that are more demanding than the moral obligations of the marketplace. There is an equally general rejection of the nation that the field of politics is a legitimate realm for private economic enrichment.

(3) "The traditionalistic political culture is rooted in an ambivalent attitude toward the marketplace coupled with a paternalistic and elitist conception of the commonwealth. It reflects an older pre-commercial attitude that accepts a substantially hierarchical society, as part of the ordered nature of things . . . . social and family ties are paramount in a traditionalistic political culture. . . . "

Clinton Rossiter's superb last Book, *The American Quest, 1790-1860,*[2] provides the most coherent account of the development process in which Elazar's individualistic mode becomes dominant.

PART II: COMPARATIVE CASE
APPROACH AND CREDIT MOBILIÉR

Just the other day I refused an offer to make ten speeches for a fee of $4,000.00 and expenses. Of course Martin Dies has followed a program of that sort but I think when he does he sells the country down the river. No one cares about hearing me speak, and the Chairman of this Committee is not for sale.

Harry S. Truman letter to Judge Schwellenbach[3]

Richard Neustadt's *Presidential Power* has demonstrated the usefulness, if not the ease, of drawing generalizations from a limited set of previously executed cases. We have summarized one such case; what can

---

[2]Clinton Rossiter, *The American Quest, 1790-1860: An Emerging Nation in Search of Identity, Unity, and Modernity* (New York: Harcourt Brace Jovanovich, 1971).

[3]Schlesinger and Bruns, 3192.

135

be learned by setting it along side a second case from the post-Civil War period? For a second case I was drawn to Credit Mobiliér. This affair has a near 100 percent recognition level, but I have yet to meet anyone who either knows what the original (French) corporation was or precisely what was thought to be so wrong about the sale, loan, or gift (the terms varied, as did the time of acquisition) of its stock to various key House and Senate members.

I would vouch to say that most of what Oakes Ames did can and is routinely done in Washington every week of the year by latter-day PAC's. In regard to the case I think it is useful to ask questions such as:

(1) What ethical positions were perceived by the major actors?

(2) By what mechanisms were facts made known?

(3) What processes and influences were involved in arriving at some sort of decision?

(4) How satisfactorily would we evaluate both the process and the final outcome?

(5) Within the cultural and political limits of the time, how might some incremental improvement in the situation have been achieved?

Perhaps more interesting questions also will occur to the reader after a brief summary of A. Schlesinger, Jr., and Roger Bruns, "The Credit Mobiliér Scandal, 1873," *Congress Investigates*, vol. 3, pp. 1849-1980.

Credit Mobiliér Stock and Complexities of Conflict of Interest

During the Civil War Congress granted charter and extensive land-grants to Union Pacific Railroad (project), with provision to take first mortgage on portions of railroad as constructed. The UP directors subsequently obtained a limited liability Penn. charter, which they renamed as "Credit Mobiliér" (name of prominent French corporation investing in various European and overseas projects). They then contracted to have their Credit Mobiliér carry out the construction but at about double the actual cost; crucial contract was signed August 9, 1867. By then it was clear that the railroad would be completed, and that the closely held Credit Mobiliér stock would be astronomically profitable: a single $100 share would, in the 12 months of 1868 alone, produce five dividends (in cash, Union Pacific shares, etc.) worth roughly $400 per share.

Railroad construction began in Iowa (where there was great public interest in the project), and much of the funding was carried out by Boston investment houses. In 1865 and 1866 the project was very short of funds and desperate efforts were made to sell stock to all and sundry.

Among those buying stock in period of 1865-66 and paying in full were:

Congressman Oakes Ames (Mass.)—leading figure in project, and chief congressional spokesman

Congressman Samuel Hooper (Mass.)—partner of investment firm in Boston

Congressman John B. Alley (Mass.), who left the House after 1866 to work for Union Pacific project

Senator James W. Grimes (Iowa), who left the Senate and died in 1872

Congressman James F. Wilson (Iowa)

Congressman (later Senator) William Boyd Allison (Iowa)

Ames said bought stock, but denying doing so:

Vice-President Schuyler Colfax (Ind.), who explained large bank deposits as resulting from unsolicited $1,000 bill (actually four of them) from a New York City well-wisher (in stationery business selling envelopes to the government; Colfax was ex-chairman of the Post Office Committee)

James A. Garfield (Ohio), who was caught in contradictions, but successfully stonewalled further investigation

Buying stock, but returning as soon as implications suggested:

Senator James A. Bayard (Del.) offered stock in December 1867 (par value), but declining:

Speaker James G. Blaine (Me.) offered and bought stock in December 1867, but returned in 1868:

Congressman Henry L. Dawes (Mass.)

Congressman Glenni W. Scofield (Pa.)

Offered and bought stock in December 1867 or 1868, but returned in 1872 (story broke as major issue in 1872 presidential election):

Congressman John A. Bingham (Ohio), who was defeated in 1872

Congressman (later Senator) John A. Logan (Ill.)

Senator Henry Wilson (Mass.) as an investment for his wife

Offered and bought stock on August 31, 1867, and defended conduct in face of Senate committee recommendation of expulsion:
Senator James Patterson (N.H.), who was not a candidate for reelection in 1872 received substantial cash from Union Pacific Vice-President Durant in 1865 for use in 1866 senate campaign (in legislature):

Congressman (later Senator) James Harlan (Iowa), admitted receiving $10,000 in 1865 for his 1866 canvass
Not offered stock by Ames, but sought out Durant and demanded shares, even though appointed as government director of Union Pacific and forbidden by statute to be a stockholder (had stock put in name of son-in-law, but dividends went to congressman):

Congressman James Brooks (N.Y.) who, like Ames, was recommended for expulsion in closing days of 42d Congress and, like Ames, died a few weeks after the investigation.
Offered stock in December 1867 and accepted on "credit" (to be paid by huge dividends):

William D. (Pig-Iron) Kelley (Pa.), who continued to serve in House until his death in 1890.

Congressional Response

House committee recommended expulsion of Ames and Brooks, but too late for action to be taken. Senate committee recommended expulsion of Patterson, also too late for action (Patterson and Ames were both leaving Congress). Ames and Brooks both died within weeks; Patterson was later elected to N.H. legislature and as Supt. of Instruction. In 1883 Mass. legislature passed resolution praising Ames and sent petition to Congress requesting like action—history has been less kind.

In contrast to the pre-Civil War pattern, the Credit Mobiliér investigation brought about no duels or violence. But neither did it bring about any very helpful reform. Scapegoats were chosen, but the correlation between extent of punishment and extent of involvement is close to zero. The issue became public only because of a falling out among the perpetrators of the scheme.

How different really are the PACs of today? For one thing there is disclosure. But beyond that most of what Elizabeth Drew complains about in her volume (based on her 1982 *New Yorker* articles) seems very comparable in essence to Credit Mobiliér. There was no exact *quid pro quo* (there seldom is); just a desire to invest funds to promote "access."

PART III: COLLECTIVE CHOICE AND INDIVIDUAL ACTION

Congressional ethics, both as reality and as public perception, constitute a "public good." But how rational is it for any member to devote scarce individual time and effort to making a small contribution to a collective good that is shared with over 500 people?

The theory of collective choice is the high-brow academic version of the individualistic ethic; it also demolishes the moralistic commitment to a "public interest" that cannot be rigorously defined.

This is not to everyone's taste. But it has the substantial merit of reminding those of us not in politics that self-interest is a very powerful factor. As a final Gedanken-experiment I would urge that we look at a case familiar to all of us in terms of what a concentration on self-interest can account for, and what remains unaccounted for (residual variance as I say on my quantitative teaching days).

My preferred case for this is Joe McCarthy and the Communist issue, 1950-1954. The thirtieth anniversary is at hand, so the younger generation may have to consult parents or the archives. Again there is an extensive documentation in *Congress Investigates*. And Nelson W. Polsby's *Commentary* article[4] neatly summarizes the literature and the conflict between those who see McCarthyism as a grass-roots movement and those who emphasize elite perception and action. Finally, Fred Greenstein has recently given us a "revisionist" view not just of Eisenhower's general political skill but in particular of his handling of the McCarthy issue.

Most of McCarthy's actions, which raised new issues as to the ethics of congressional investigations, would seem to have been rational once you accept a desire for publicity and an unusual willingness to take risks. Neither the Senate nor the media were quite prepared for someone who was

---

[4]Nelson W. Polsby, "Down Memory Lane with Joe McCarthy," *Commentary*, vol. 75, no. 2 (1983): 55-59.

so incautious, so lacking in what a collective choice analyst would regard as risk aversion.

What best accounts for the behavior of the 95 other senators? Was it self-interest typical of the individualistic culture? There were a handful of moralists. But if Greenstein is right in his *The Hidden-Hand Presidency*, they may have been helping to promote McCarthy, just as Ohio Congressman Stanberry helped to put Sam Houston back in the spotlight.

What were the conditions that finally brought a majority of the Senate to move against McCarthy? Could he have been checked earlier? Could that sort of thing happen again?

CONCLUDING THOUGHTS

The dominance of the individualistic mode in the 20th century strongly suggests a rather limited role for congressional ethics. Most of the public for most of the time is simply not going to demand the sort of behavior that a moralistic subculture would seek to enforce. The practical problem, then, is one of consolidating the modest gains of the past decade. The establishment of formal committees on ethics (or official standards) is a very significant improvement in many ways. Yet one does not have to be a very close observer to recognize that these committees are very fragile institutions, offering virtually no positive attractions to members, and open to criticism (e.g., dealing in minutia, although even this can be helpful). The more one reads of the awkwardness, bumbling, and partisanship that dominated most investigations in the 19th century the more one appreciates the gains of recent years. It would be helpful to have a monograph detailing what the House and Senate ethics committees (to use the generic term) *have* managed to do. Devising ways to strengthen these institutions may be more important than drafting "the" ideal ethics code—something attractive only to a minority of moralists.

One "lesson" of history is the difficulty of establishing a given ethical criteria in the face of strongly entrenched competing criteria. This is not to embrace William Graham Sumner's "folkways" as the whole story, but to recognize that a moralistic culture accepted by one-fourth of the country (and Congress) will find it difficult to prescribe behavior for the 50 percent who are individualistic, or the remaining one-fourth who are Traditional. The current effort to develop more acceptable limits on PACs is likely to be as long and tortuous as, say, the elimination of physical violence and dueling in the pre-Civil War Congress.

A second "lesson" is the importance of establishing regular machinery for monitoring problem areas and routinely investigating charges. Congress, the House in particular, did this for contested elections in its first decade. But for ethics more broadly construed this is a development of the past 20 years. One has only contrast the handling of the recent Studds-Crane sex scandals with what would have occurred if the matter had been left to individual charges and partisan maneuvering. Institutions or committees may need strengthening but they are a vast improvement over no institution at all.

Chapter 7

New Perspectives on Wilson's Congressional Government

It is over a century now since Woodrow Wilson published *Congressional Government*. In the final paragraph of that work he reminds us that "the Constitution is not honored by blind worship." Perhaps it is time to say the same thing for Wilson's most famous book. The young Wilson's goals, like those of a congressman, were multiple. He needed a dissertation to obtain his degree, he wanted to produce a publishable manuscript, and he sought to convince his readers of the superiority of British style cabinet government to the existing pattern of American government (as he viewed it). The Johns Hopkins University authorities were remarkably cooperative in regard to the first goal, and Houghton Mifflin publishers were agreeable in regard to the second. In retrospect the third goal seems utopian, but the book was respectfully received and for a time did generate the sort of discussion that Wilson sought. But after a few years it might be expected to have dropped out of sight.

Why is Wilson's hastily written dissertation, which was based on little or no serious research either in primary sources or first-hand Washington observation still widely read (or at least quoted) and regarded as a classic? Wilson's concern for style and his eye for the apt phrase (our modern "soundbite") are part of the story. And his subsequent rise to the presidency guarantees a certain interest in his earlier writings. But I would suggest that there are two additional reasons for continued interest in *Congressional*

Government.[1] First, though Wilson failed to make a dent in American constitutional practices by his book, he did strike a rich vein of continuing interest in the comparison of British and American political practices. For this, as well as for the general approach and analytic tone of the book, Wilson had Walter Bagehot to thank.

In *The English Constitution* Bagehot concludes:

> The practical choice of first-rate nations is between the *Presidential* government and the Parliamentary; no State can be first-rate which has not a government by discussion, and those are the only two existing species of that government. It is between them that a nation which has to choose its government must choose.[2]

In the "Preface" to *Congressional Government* Wilson significantly tips his hand by shifting the comparison as follows:

> The most striking contrast in modern politics is not between presidential and monarchical governments, but between *Congressional* and Parliamentary governments. Congressional Government is Committee government; Parliamentary government is government by a responsible Cabinet Ministry. These are the two principal types which present themselves for the instruction of the modern student of the practical in politics. . . .[3]

By labeling the American system "congressional" rather than "presidential" Wilson seeks to wish away the separation of powers and narrow the comparison to alternative schemes of legislative supremacy. But whatever the labels, the comparison of the two systems has remained a fascinating subject on down to the Thatcher-Reagan era.

But there is a second and more important reason for the continued interest in and citation of *Congressional Government*, even among straightforward students of American politics. I would like to explore the hypothesis that Wilson's devastating strictures on disjointed committees sound

---

[1] All cites to Wilson in this chapter are from Woodrow Wilson, *Congressional Government: A Study in American Politics* (Cleveland: Meridian Books, 1956).

[2] Walter Bagehot, *The English Constitution* (London: King, 1872 ed.), 311-12.

[3] Wilson, 24.

amazingly on target for the seniority-based committees of mid 20th-century America precisely because he was way off-base, inaccurate, or inconsistent in his treatment of committees and leaders of the Congress of his own day (the 1880s). In short, he managed to be spectacularly wrong about the 19th-century Congress, but in ways that happen to become peculiarly *appropriate* for the post-1911 Congress! If he had done a more careful job on the Congress of his own time I suspect he would be of very limited interest to the current generation of students of Congress.

The case for this somewhat unorthodox view is presented in three parts. The first examines the often overlooked major thesis of *Congressional Government*. The second part presents the case in regard to committees and leaders. The third part then broadens the analysis to ask what authors were more successful than Wilson in detailing 19th-century political realities, and how Wilson reacted to such alternatives.

I.

For all practical purposes the national government is supreme over the state governments, and Congress is predominant over its so called coordinate branches. Whereas Congress at first overshadowed neither president nor federal judiciary, it now on occasion rules both with easy mastery and with a high hand.[4]

Congressional Government is usually praised as the first major book about Congress and its committees. But Wilson's clear intention was to write a book about the American political system in general, just as Bagehot had written about British politics in general. It turns out to be a book mostly about the Congress because Wilson—a southerner—took the results of what he terms the "war between the states" to mean the virtual supremacy of the federal government over the states, and in Washington the almost total sway of Congress over the president and Supreme Court. The useless "literary theory" that Wilson wants to sweep away is nothing less than the whole set of constitutional checks and balances of 1787! If such a radical change had occurred then the system would indeed be ripe for Wilson's pet prescription of cabinet government.

---

[4]Wilson, 53-54.

If there was an American writer of the time with experience and insight to rival that of Walter Bagehot it was Henry Adams. In 1870 Adams had noted the contrast between the American founders' fear of concentrated power and demand for checks and balances with the European belief in ultimate sovereignty, that "supreme irresistible authority must exist somewhere in every government. . . . " He continues:

> The two great theories of government stood face to face during three-quarters of a century. Europe still maintained that supreme power must be trusted to every government, democratic or not, and America still maintained that such a principle was inconsistent with freedom. The civil war broke out in the United States, and of course for the time obliterated the Constitution. Peace came, and with it came the moment for the final settlement of this long scientific dispute. If the constitutional system restored itself, America was right, and the oldest problem in political science was successfully solved.[5]

Wilson simply assumes the answer to this experiment, and proclaims the European view: "There is always a centre of power: where in this system is that centre?" What the pessimistic Adams feared might occur in the long run has already occurred in the view of the young Wilson who concludes:

> It is said that there is no single or central force in our federal scheme; and so there is not in the federal scheme. . . . How is it, however, in the practical conduct of the federal government? In that, unquestionably, the predominant and controlling force, the centre and source of all motive and of all regulative power, is Congress. All niceties of constitutional restriction and even many broad principles of constitutional limitation have been overridden. . . .[6]

As early as the fifth paragraph of his introductory chapter Wilson makes explicit that "the actual form of our present government is simply a scheme of congressional supremacy."[7] *This* is Wilson's major thesis to which the role of uncoordinated standing committees is merely a corollary.

---

[5]We have been unable to find the source of this quote (editor).
[6]Wilson, 30-31.
[7]*Ibid.*, 28.

This is an incredible line of analysis. Wilson writes as if Thaddeus Stevens and his Radical Wing of the post-Civil War Republican party had indeed driven President Andrew Johnson from office and taken over Washington. But Johnson survived, and the Radicals soon faced a loss of public support. For most of the period 1868-1885 the question was more one of Senate hegemony versus Republican presidents, the issue being control of appointments and consequently of the party organization. But Wilson has little or no interest in the Senate and no sympathy for Republican Presidents Hayes, Arthur, and Garfield, who managed to regain most of the ground lost by Johnson and Grant.

Two factors seem to have moved Wilson to his extreme view of congressional omnipotence. We know that his great aim was to move American politics in the direction of cabinet government. Now if congressional supremacy had already been brought about by the extraconstitutional changes of the Civil War and Reconstruction then the road to adoption of cabinet government is wide open. Not even a formal constitutional amendment would be needed, or at most a few words changed to permit congressmen to hold an additional office.

But for opening the door to cabinet government it was Wilson's own beloved South that had paid a very heavy price. Congress, he writes, had used its implied powers to extend "into every community of the land a sense of federal power." He continues: "Who does not feel that the [federal] marshal represents a greater power than the sheriff does, and that it is more dangerous to molest a mail carrier [federal] than to knock down a policeman?" Then we get to the heart of Wilson's complaint:

> Whilst federal postmasters are valued . . . and whilst very few people realize the weight of customs-duties . . . everybody eyes rather uneasily the federal supervisors at the polls. . . . The federal supervisor, consequently, who oversees the balloting for congressmen, practically superintends the election of state officers also. . . . The supervisor represents the very ugliest side of federal supremacy; he belongs to the least liked branch of the civil service; but his existence speaks very clearly as to the present balance of powers, and his rather hateful privileges must, under the present system of mixed [federal and state] elections, result in

impairing the self-respect of state officers of election by bringing home to them a vivid sense of subordination to the powers of Washington.[8]

This is a theme that Wilson had expressed in his undergraduate days at Princeton, as in the following marginal comment (right side) written in one of his texts (left side):

Text: "If the Wars of the Roses failed in utterly destroying English freedom, they succeeded in arresting its progress for more than a hundred years. With them we enter on an epoch of constitutional retrogression in which the slow work of the age that went before it was rapidly undone." (John Richard Green, *History of the English People*, Vol. II [New York: The Useful Knowledge Publishing Company, 1882]).

Wilson notes: The wars of the Roses and the Civil war in America issued in results not altogether dissimilar: with the triumph of the House of York unrestrained and irresponsible power passed into the hands of the royal Council; with the death of the Confederate cause in America unrestrained and irresponsible power began to be exercised by Congress; thus creating a nursery for corruption and threatening death to free institutions.

Wilson has further complaints about "the tide of federal aggression" but they all lead to the conclusion that "the balances of the Constitution are for the most part only ideal." This indicates what a study of the "real" American constitutional system should concentrate on:

As the House of Commons is the central object of examination in every of the English Constitution, so should Congress be in every study of our own.[9]

In his chapter titles Wilson carries this out with a vengeance. First comes the crucial "introductory" chapter with its overview. It is followed by two long chapters on the House, comprising almost half the book. This is followed by a short chapter on the Senate. The president is submerged in a short chapter on "The Executive." The Supreme Court does not warrant even a short chapter.

---

[8]*Ibid.*, 39-40.
[9]*Ibid.*, 53, 56.

The mature Wilson knew better. In his *Constitutional Government in the United States* (1908) there are chapters of approximately equal length, starting with the president, followed by the House, the Senate, and the Courts. But there is also a chapter on the states and the federal government, and a new chapter on party government. In 1885 Wilson simply lacked the experience and contacts to become the American Bagehot. Indeed, it would be another dozen years before there was to be a book on American politics that one might reasonably put in a class with Bagehot's on English politics (see Part III).

But Christopher Columbus failed of his expressed goal, the East Indies, and we respect him for what he did accomplish. If Wilson is no American Bagehot he has a strong claim to academic discovery of congressional committees and their vital role. It is to this topic that we now turn.

II.

> The extinction of the committee system must appear certain to any one who will seriously contemplate the future of the Union. . . .
> . . . Committee government cannot last, whatever other system be substituted.[10]

The enduring interest in Wilson's book rests not on the spurious claim of congressional supremacy in a unitary state, but on the pungency and relevance of his many statements about congressional committees:

> The House sits, not for serious discussion, but to sanction the conclusions of its Committees as rapidly as possible. It legislates in its committee rooms . . . so that it is not far from the truth to say that Congress in session is Congress on public exhibition, whilst Congress in its committee rooms is Congress at work.[11]

Here we have a basic insight, brilliantly stated, and much quoted. Since committees are not mentioned in the Constitution, Wilson is moving here

---

[10]Woodrow Wilson, "Government by Debate," in *The Papers of Woodrow Wilson,* ed. Arthur S. Link (Princeton: Princeton University Press, 1967), II, 271, 273.

[11]Wilson, *Congressional Government,* 69.

into the "reality" of extraconstitutional practice. The functional advantages of a committee system are many: for Wilson committees were dysfunctional since they stood in the way of his desire for responsible party leaders to function by means of oratory from the floor.

That Congress does most of its works in committees was hardly news in 1885; Wilson notes that George Frisbie Hoar (former House member and subsequently senator) had previously termed them "little legislatures." To support his thesis Wilson might have quoted comments by House members such as the following:

> In every legislature, the introduction, progress and conclusion of business depend much upon committees; and, in the House of Representatives of the U.S., more than in any other legislative body within my knowledge, the business referred to Committees, and reported on by them, is, by usage and common consent, controlled by their chairman. As the Speaker, according to the standing rules of the House, has the appointment of Committees, he has it in his power to place whom he pleases in the foreground, and whom he pleases in the background, and thus, in some measure, affect their agency in the transactions of the House.

"Thus wrote Barnabas Bidwell to President Jefferson in 1806," Cunningham comments, "more than three-quarters of a century before Wilson wrote his book!"[12]

What Wilson objects to is, first, that "the proceedings of the Committees are private and their discussions unpublished."[13] Real debate is thus shifted "from the floor of Congress to the privacy of the committee rooms."[14] And this reduces public interest and undermines public accountability. Wilson gives us a sort of syllogism, based on the need for public accountability:

(1) Congress does it real work in committee, not on the floor.

(2) But congressional committees meet in private.

---

[12]Noble E. Cunningham, Jr., *The Jeffersonian Republicans in Power: Party Operations, 1801-1809* (Williamsburg, Va.: University of North Carolina Press, 1963), 90-91.

[13]Wilson, *Congressional Quarterly,* 71.

[14]*Ibid.,* 70.

(3) Therefore, we should abolish committees and admit cabinet officers to appear on the floor (or appoint members to serve in the cabinet).

This would seem both faulty logic and a classic example of throwing the baby out with the bath. Why not open congressional committee meetings to public scrutiny? Wilson rather lamely cites questionable precedent against publication of committee proceedings. He goes on to argue that on the rare occasions when outside witnesses do appear before a committee the result is mere special pleading, not principled debated.[15]

Wilson does not consider the counter-syllogism that goes:

(1) Congress does its real work in committees, not on the floor.

(2) Cabinet officers should publicly defend their proposals where Congress does it real work.

(3) Therefore, cabinet officers should appear in committee hearings that are open to the public and press.

This, of course, is what in fact has happened. The route and pace by which it has come about, however, are almost entirely unstudied and would constitute a fascinating research project.

Wilson's second great complaint about committees is that in both chambers power is dispersed among a large number of committee chairmen, and the result is confusion and lack of responsibility. The debater in Wilson takes charge, and he is carried away with the sheer charm of his own words:

> Our legislation is conglomerate, not homogenous. The doings of one and the same Congress are foolish in pieces and wise in spots. They can never, except by accident, have any common feature. Some of the Committees are made up of strong men, the majority of them of weak men, and the weak are as influential as the strong.[16]

Then he fires a final mighty salvo:

> There could be no more interesting problem in the doctrine of chances than that of reckoning the probabilities of there being any common features of principle in the legislation of an opening session. It

---

[15]*Ibid.*, 72.
[16]*Ibid.*, 89.

might lighten and divert the leisure of some ingenious mathematician to attempt the calculation.[17]

Surely that settles the matter.

But wait—what of the Speaker, who appoints all chairmen and committee members at his discretion (until 1911)? Since the Speaker presides and is not on the floor leading the oratorical struggle Wilson is dubious. "He appoints the leaders of the House, but he is not himself its leader."[18] This is a handsome sentence, but sadly deficient in political understanding. Throughout the book Wilson has a strange blind spot in regard to the power resulting from the ability to appoint and remove others from office. In regard both to the president (who appoints his cabinet) and the House Speaker (who appoints his committee chairmen and members) Wilson disdains the appointing power as a seemingly trivial matter:

> From the necessity of the case, however, the President cannot often be really supreme in matters of administration, except as the Speaker of the House of Representatives is supreme in legislation, as appointer of those who are supreme in its several departments.[19]

In the case of the presidency Wilson comes to a stunning conclusion:

> Except in so far as his power of veto constitutes him apart of the legislature, the President might, not inconveniently, be a permanent officer: the first official of a carefully graded and impartially regulated civil service system. . . . He is part of the official rather than of the political machinery of the government. . . .[20]

But the importance of the Speaker is just too great to overlook so Wilson is soon off on the opposite tack. Instead of uncoordinated committees we have the "imperial" Speakership:

> It is highly interesting to note the extraordinary power accruing to Mr. Speaker through this pregnant prerogative of appointing the Standing

---

[17]*Ibid.*
[18]*Ibid.,* 58.
[19]*Ibid.,*173.
[20]*Ibid.,* 170.

Committees of the House. . . . The most esteemed writers upon our Constitution have failed to observe, not only that the Standing Committees are the most essential machinery of our governmental system, but also that the Speaker of the House of Representative is the most powerful functionary of that system. So sovereign is he within the wide sphere of his influence that one could wish for accurate knowledge as to the actual extent of his power. . . . All Speakers have, of late years especially, been potent factors in legislation, but some have, by reason of greater energy or less conscience, made more use of their opportunities than have others.[21]

The Speaker, then, "is an autocrat of the first magnitude," and the office "a constitutional phenomenon of the first importance." When there is a contest for the Speakership there is "intense interest excited throughout the country as to the choice to be made." And small wonder: "If there be differences of opinion within the party, a choice between leaders becomes a choice between policies and assumes the greatest significance." Wilson summarizes the result:

Of late years, the newspapers have had almost as much to say about the rival candidates for that office [Speaker] as about the rival candidates for the presidency itself, having come to look upon the selection made as a sure index of the policy to be expected in legislation.[22]

Between pages 85 and 89 we go from a "sure index of policy" to "the doctrine of chances." You pay your money and take your choice. . .

Now it is clear as to which of these rival images is more accurate. Speakers Colfax and Blaine on the Republican side and Randall and Carlisle on the Democratic side were strong and effective leaders and generally recognized as such. They had not taken the Speakership quite to the peaks of power and controversy associated with Reed or Cannon. The 1880 revision of the House Rules, which Wilson seems unaware of, had made the Rules Committee a standing committee and broadened its power. In the very Congress that met while Wilson was writing (1883-84), Speaker

---

[21]*Ibid.,* 83.
[22]*Ibid.,* 85.

Carlisle named the chairmen of Ways and Means and of Appropriations to serve with him on the majority side of the Rules Committee.[23]

But Wilson cannot opt for the accurate image of an effective party and a policy-oriented Speaker. This would totally undermine the whole thrust of his book and render irrelevant most of his most quotable quotes. When the quotes *do* become relevant is after the 1910-1911 "syndication" of the Speakership, and the emergence of a clear norm of systematic seniority in the House. This occurred, ironically enough, during Woodrow Wilson's presidency. The result by the 1930s was indeed disjointed and dispersed committee control. It was anti-New Deal southern Democratic chairman and the "conservative coalition" (Republican plus a majority of southern Democrats) who gave real meaning to Wilson's jeremiad of half a century earlier.

What a marvelous target "seniority" would have made for the young Wilson. Here indeed was a seemingly irrational system based on the sheerest accident of longevity and assignment, with no regard to merit or policy view. And it was virtually guaranteed to produce a highly dispersed set of committee chairmen, with no common viewpoint. But Wilson never even dreamed of the possibility of such a system, much less that it was largely in place for the Senate at the very time that he was writing.[24]

After World war II we begin to get a substantial body of serious research on Congress. Not surprisingly most of this research emphasizes the role of committees, organized on the basis of seniority.[25] For this there is no more relevant and sparkling chapter headnote or inspiring quote, selectively chosen, than *Congressional Government*. But what an ironic immortality this is. Wilson hated committees with a consuming passion and had little interest in how they worked or in their relations with the overall chamber. The problem as he saw it was that they existed at all.

In December 1889 Wilson wrote in his "confidential journal": "No man can appreciate a parliament who would not make a useful member of

---

[23]*Ibid.*

[24]Randall B. Ripley, *Power in the Senate* (New York: St. Martins Press, 1969), 42.

[25]Richard F. Fenno, *The Power of the Purse: Appropriations Politics in Congress* (Boston: Little, Brown, & Co., 1966).

it. . . .[26] No one can give a true account of anything of which he is intolerant." The careful reader of *Congressional Government* will recognize the truth of this judgment. Yet Wilson stands a century later as the unchallenged patron saint and founding father of the serious academic study of committees. It is a fate he certainly did not seek.

III.

> Mr. Ford is the first of the students of American politics to perceive and
> to state clearly the position which the American political party occupies
> in American political life.[27]

We all recognize that American government does not function along the classic "literary" lines of the theory of 1787. The separation of powers has been substantially modified, although not by the means that Wilson recommended. Thus we are faced with three final questions in connection with *Congressional Government*. First, in the absence of congressional supremacy or cabinet government, what has been the chief trend in extra-constitutional development? Second, who can lay claim to being the American equivalent of Bagehot by developing the first sustained analysis of the change "realities" of American politics? And, lastly, how does Woodrow Wilson respond to the awkward situation of someone else solving the broad problem that he had posed, but failed to solve, in *Congressional Government*?

Surely the single most important development over the first century of operation of the Constitution was the development of mass political parties, what Arthur Holcombe aptly termed the "unplanned institutional of organized partisanship." The rise of parties was facilitated by the growth of a more democratic political culture and by Andrew Jackson's redefinition of the presidency as a sort of tribune of the people. In the last quarter of the 19th century the role of political parties was simply too great to ignore, as Wilson did. The workings of the party system and of public opinion was of central importance to such writers as James Bryce (*The American Common-*

---

[26]Link, ed., vol. 6, 463.

[27]Frank J. Goodnow, review of Henry Jones Ford, *The Rise and Growth of American Politics, Political Science Quarterly*, vol. 14, no. 1 (1899): 155-57.

Wealth, two volumes), A. Lawrence Lowell, and M. Ostrogorski (*Democracy and the Organization of Political Parties*, separate volumes on the United States and on Great Britain).

But the most incisive treatment of the subject (in my view and in the view of Woodrow Wilson) came from Henry Jones Ford. In 1898 Ford, a longtime newspaperman and editor, published *The Rise and Growth of American Politics.*[28] Like Wilson, Ford was concerned with the problem of public accountability and fascinated by extraconstitutional change. But unlike the young Wilson, Ford found the key to both in the rise of mass political parties, and especially in the Jacksonian development of the presidency as "a representative institution" (his chapter XV). His emphasis on the presidency was especially insightful for an author writing in the 1890s (like Wilson again, Ford was an admirer of the strong-willed Grover Cleveland). Ford's analysis remains well worth reading today.

Henry Jones Ford could well claim to have done for American politics what Walter Bagehot had done some three decades earlier for English politics: he had gone behind the forms of government to show how things really worked, and why (Ford emphasizes self-interest, with responsibility to the public as a by-product). But one might well wonder, how does Wilson react to this startlingly different analysis that solves the problem that had so preoccupied the young Wilson?

It is a pleasure to report that Wilson's response to Ford's analysis was enthusiastic. No matter that it made hash of most of what Wilson had written some dozen years earlier. Wilson was a big enough man to be more concerned that there be a solution to the problem of generating leadership with public accountability than that the solution be his own favorite. He doubtless had come to recognize that Bagehot had been right in classifying presidential and parliamentary systems as two different species. Given the American constitution, cabinet government was simply out of the question. But effective and responsible public leadership was possible. It was not a guaranteed outcome, but it could be achieved by means of a strong president who effectively led public opinion and his party. And national events, such as the increased importance of foreign affairs (Spanish-American War) and the example of Theodore Roosevelt in the White

---

[28]Henry Jones Ford, *The Rise and Growth of American Politics* (New York: The Macmillan Co., 1898).

House, soon reinforced the cogency of Ford's brilliant analysis. For Princeton students Wilson now suggested that *Congressional Government* (which posed the problem) was "to be read along with Henry Jones Ford, *The Rise and Growth of American Politics*" (which provided an alternative solution). What greater praise than that?

Actually, Wilson went further, much further. Although Ford was a practicing newspaper man with no graduate training and an undergraduate degree from lowly Baltimore City Colleges, Wilson set about bringing Ford to Princeton as a professor of politics! Nothing came of this in 1899-1900, but several years later Ford became interested in a move from Pittsburgh (his newspaper base) back to the East Coast and also a move into academic life. Wilson again was enthusiastic. He saw to it that a Princeton offer was made, which Ford accepted. Small wonder that Wilson's 1908 book starts with a chapter on the president and includes a lengthy analysis of "party government!" The two became close friends. After his entry into elective politics Wilson brought Ford into his administration both in New Jersey and later in Washington, D.C.

Woodrow Wilson was a man of passionate and sometimes stubborn conviction. Obviously he never entirely outgrew his early fascination with cabinet government. But after his 1898 encounter with Ford he recognized that American politics had a different logic. Wilson accepted the nomination for governor of New Jersey from a political machine of the sort that Ford had so brilliantly analyzed. And in the "elective kingship" (as Ford termed it) of the presidency, Wilson added a whole new chapter to our understanding of presidential leadership.

It remains only to point out that it was during Wilson's presidency that effective party control of House committees gradually lost hold (following the 1910-1911 dismantling of the strong Speakership). By roughly 1920 the seniority system was as sacred a standard in the House as it had become in the 1880s for the Senate. As a result, and quite by accident, Wilson's youthful jibes about disjointed policy and irresponsible committees were suddenly to acquire new relevance. But perhaps we should follow the mature Wilson's advice and assign along with *Congressional Government* the more realistic emphasis on party and presidency that was added by his friend and colleague Henry Jones Ford. For this country has never had congressional government.

III. Methods of Inquiry

Chapter 8

Are Southern Democrats Different?
An Application of Scale Analysis
to Senate Voting Patterns

INTRODUCTION

In any given period a discipline possesses certain resources of knowledge, experience, and imagination. These resources are sufficient to deal with some problems, but not with others. An eminent mathematician puts the matter this way:

> Imagine farmers living in a country where no other tool was available except the wooden plough. Of necessity, the farms would have to be in those places where the earth was soft enough to be cultivated with a wooden implement. If the population grew sufficiently to occupy every suitable spot, the farms would become a map of the soft earth regions. If anyone ventured beyond this region, he would perish and leave no trace. It is much the same with mathematical research.[1]

This article originally appeared in *Politics and Social Life: An Introduction to Political Behavior,* ed. Nelson W. Polsby, Robert A. Dentler, and Paul A. Smith (Boston: Houghton Mifflin, 1963), 740-56.
[1]W. W. Sawyer, *Prelude to Mathematics* (Harmondsworth, Middlesex: Penguin, 1955), 64.

And, one might add, with the social sciences. The map of our reliable knowledge—as distinguished from speculations or hunches—does come to resemble the map of those problems that can be handled by our existing tools and techniques. Other problems may be raised, and be of great importance, but without appropriate research tools they cannot be answered in an adequate manner.

Among the more fascinating problems for the student of internal party processes is the question of "who votes with whom, and on what" in the Congress. Unfortunately, few tools for readily tackling this problem have been available, hence it has remained pretty much off the map of our reliable knowledge. In fact, over the past 25 years—since the pioneering studies of Stuart Rice and Herman Beyle—there has been a surprising lack of innovation in quantitative techniques for the study of the legislative process. This paper seeks to explore the research implications of a relatively new technique, Louis Guttman's scale analysis, which the author has applied in a more general study of Senate voting patterns over the period 1949-1956.[2] In this paper particular emphasis is placed upon problems of intraparty adjustment, using southern and nonsouthern Senate Democrats as an example.

This paper is divided into three parts. In Part I three major alternative approaches to the systematic analysis of roll call votes are contrasted, and some limitations on the usefulness of each are indicated. In Part II the methodology of scaling is very briefly explained, and its relation to Professor Beyle's attribute-cluster-bloc analysis explained. In Part III, finally, some substantive results of the application of scaling to Senate voting are presented.

---

[2]H. D. Price, "Scale Analysis of Senate Voting Patterns, 1949-1956" (Unpublished Ph.D. thesis, Harvard University, 1958). The author is indebted to the SSRC for a predoctoral training fellowship in support of the research, and to Professor V. O. Key, Jr., for his suggestions and encouragement. Other applications of scaling to analysis of legislative voting include: George M. Belknap, "A Method for Analyzing Legislative Behavior," *Midwest Journal of Political Science,* II (1958): 377-402; Charles D. Farris, "A Method of Determining Ideological Groupings in the Congress," *Journal of Politics* 20 (1958): 308-38; and Duncan MacRae, Jr., *Dimensions of Congressional Voting* (Berkeley and Los Angeles: University of California Press, 1958).

I.

No statistical analysis can rise to greater significance than the data on which it is based. Now there are certain obvious limitations on the value of roll call votes as basic data. Certainly a simple "yea" or "nay" vote cannot express differing degrees of intensity of feeling, doubts about different parts of a complex measure, and may conceal the fact that the same response may come from two legislators for contradictory reasons (as in the not too frequent situation where two extremes join to defeat a compromise proposal). Further, there is considerable evidence that a legislator's own personal opinion or the position he takes within committee may well differ from the stand he takes on a record vote. One even hears rumors that on occasion votes are more or less traded, as when some western Democrats vote with the southerners on civil rights in return for needed southern support for a high federal dam in Hell's Canyon. Despite these limitations roll call votes are of great importance in the legislative struggle and, properly used, are a very valuable source of data.

In addition to the worth of the basic data the value of any quantitative study is also limited by the validity of the techniques by which the data is handled. This second sort of problem, involving the logical analysis of the quantification process, has not been the subject of much attention among political scientists.[3] Most quantitative roll call studies can be said to follow one or another of three general approaches that correspond rather closely to the three classic positions on the age-old philosophical question of the existence of universals (Plato's "ideas," the abstract entities of the Middle Ages, and abstract classes in general). The differing assumptions of these three positions, which are summarized in Table 1 below, are of direct relevance for this study and will be briefly contrasted.

1. *Research Nominalism.* Taking the last-named approach of Table 1 first, the research nominalist steers clear of numerical indexes of such abstract entities as "liberalism" or "isolationism." Refusing to deal with such abstractions the nominalist will usually regard each roll call vote as a unique irreducible event. He may count the number of different instances

---

[3]Honorable exceptions here are the careful work done by Herbert A. Simon on the measurement of "power," by James G. March on the Measurement of "influence," and by Robert A. Dahl on democratic theory.

Table 1. *Characteristics of Alternative Approaches to Statistical Roll Call Analysis*

Type of Approach	Level of Analysis	Ontological Commitment	Type of Measurement Used
Research Neoplatonism	Ideologies or other broad "isms"	Universals exist in nature	In cardinal numbers (e.g., "60% liberal")
Research Conceptualism	Middle-range policy attitudes	Universals are mind-made categories	In ordinal rankings
Research Nominalism	Individual roll calls of specific issues	Minimize use of universals	Usually none, though classification may be used

in which a given proportion of southern Democrats vote with the Republican majority, but he will never, never—or at least hardly ever—try to combine these votes into some high-level composite variable. This cautious approach, embodying the minimum ontological commitments and giving the maximum regard to the integrity of the basic data, characterizes much of the work of such outstanding students as V. O. Key and Julius Turner. Needless to say, this approach has much to commend it though it may require an unusual talent for generalizing to be able to draw any simple conclusions from its mass of data.

2. *Research Neoplatonism.* This position is at the opposite extreme. And as Moliere's M. Jourdain went through life speaking "prose" without ever realizing it, so some researchers are perhaps equally unwitting users of the Neoplatonic doctrine that universals or abstractions (such as "liberalism" and "isolationism") do exist in nature. Most researchers do not trouble themselves with this implicit assumption, but set right out to measure these

abstract variables, and to measure them by *cardinal* numbers.[4] Given some multisyllable "ism," the research Neoplatonist will collect a batch of roll call votes that might conceivably be said to have some relation to the broad topic and compute each individual senator's arithmetic percentage of support. The resulting index scores are then analyzed in terms of supposed cardinal values measured from a supposed zero point along the supposed dimension. This, needless to say, involves a lot of supposition!

Now the research nominalist *may* be open to some criticism for sticking too closely to the data and not exploiting those further regularities that might be found, but the research Neoplatonist *must* be criticized for allowing imagination to run beserk. Both the identification of a single variable and the development of a quantitative metric are complex tasks. The ordinary numerical index number of legislative attitudes, however, is usually put together in such a manner that it violates some of the most basic rules of logic and mathematics (though perhaps not necessarily those of common sense, since the results may be of some rough value in pointing up gross differences).

The basic objection to the research Neoplatonist's type of "measurement" is that it puts the cart (of quantification in cardinal values) before determining if there is a horse (a cumulative rank order along which a measurement might be made). Now a quantitative measurement of a variable implies the prior existence of a specific cumulative rank order.[5] Our number system by its very definition is cumulative and implies the existence of a rank order. Hence any variable to which numbers are

---

[4]The distinction between *cardinal* numbers (one, two, three, etc., which assert numerical values) and *ordinal* numbers (first, second, third, etc., which indicate only relative position) is of vital importance. It is not, as sometimes suggested by language students, something invented to make the mastery of French or German more difficult.

[5]For excellent discussion of this topic see Carl G. Hempel, *Fundamentals of Concept Formation in Empirical Science,* International Encyclopedia of Unified Science, vol. 2, no. 7, especially pages 50-69; Gustav Bergmann and Kenneth W. Spence, "The Logic of Psychophysical Measurement," *Psychological Review* (1944), reprinted in *Readings in the Philosophy of Science,* ed. Herbert Feigl and May Brodbeck (New York: Appleton-Century-Crofts, 1953), 103-19; and S. S. Stevens, "Mathematics, Measurement, and Psychophysics," in *Handbook of Experimental Psychology,* ed. S. S. Stevens (New York: Wiley, 1951), 1-49.

meaningfully applied must also be cumulative. And if cardinal numbers are applied then that variable must have a given zero point and a basic unit of measure in which all differences of degree can be expressed.

The fallacy of most shortcuts to the cardinal measurement of legislators' attitudes lies in the failure to test whether the various individual votes in an index can be shown to relate to a *single* possible variable and to a cumulative rank order. Contrast the concepts of "height" and "liberalism" for example. Every senator who is at least as tall as the 6' mark in height is also at least as tall as the 5' 11" mark, the 5' 10" mark, and every other lesser mark. But if he is "80 percent liberal" on the basis of a 10-vote index can we guarantee that he voted for at least every included bill for which a "60 percent liberal" voted? Generally we cannot. In fact, we may even find that "50 percent liberal" Jones voted liberal on issues 1, 3, 5, 7, and 9 while "50 percent liberal" Smith voted liberal on issues 2, 4, 6, 8, and 10.

But this is surely incredible. Two individuals with supposedly identical degrees of the attribute under study might be opposed on all of the issues included in the index. Now one never finds two five-inch long pencils such that each reaches five of the inch-markers on a 10-inch ruler, but one reaches only the odd-numbered markers while the other reaches only the even ones! It is not enough to merely reach *any* five markers—if we are to genuinely measure a single variable then they must be the first five markers in an ordered series, and they must include all those markers reached by any object of lesser length and be included in those reached by any object of greater length. And so it is—or should be—with votes used in an index. If they are to genuinely measure a single variable then they must constitute a cumulative series of more and more stringent tests of the variable, thus dividing the population under study into cumulative groups.[6]

---

[6]For some purposes and under specified conditions it may be useful to develop a composite index number that deliberately involves several different dimensions. Thus the composite "cost-of-living index" may remain constant while farm prices fall and industrial goods increase in price. Such a composite is of some use because each item can be weighted in terms of a common denominator—namely, the dollar—and the prices of an identical "market-basket of goods" can be compared for different periods. Unfortunately, an index of "liberalism" is not so useful since there is no generally accepted common denominator for weighting the importance of, say civil rights in comparison to farm legislation, nor does each year bring up a fixed number of votes in the different areas. One year there will be many votes

3.   *Research Conceptualism.* Fortunately there is a middle position that sympathizes with the nominalists' respect for the integrity of the data, but which also shares the Neoplatonists' urge for more general categories of analysis. Conceptualism differs from the Neoplatonists' position in that it denies that there are universals or abstract entities in nature waiting to be discovered, holding rather that such concepts are more or less useful man-made "inventions." At a more down to earth level the conceptualism should be a popular as well as a respectable position since, as Harvard's W. V. Quine points out, "the tired nominalist can lapse into conceptualism and still allay his puritanic conscience that he has not quite taken to eating lotus with the platonists."[7]

In roll call analysis the research conceptualist seeks to combine individual votes in such a manner that the existence of various more general underlying variables (or dimensions) can be suggested as a logical possibility (though not a certainty) and so that individual legislators can be compared in an ordinal (that is, rank order) manner in regard to such hypothetical variables. Thus the conceptualist seeks to go beyond the rather strict limits of research nominalism, but without being forced to embrace the illogic of research Neoplatonism. One technique for doing this is by use of Louis Guttman's scale analysis. In the course of the past decade a sizeable literature has developed on the subject of scalings,[8] but the basic concept and its particular importance for roll call analysis are briefly summarized in the following section.

---

on civil rights and perhaps none on farm policy; the next year the situation may be the reverse. An index based on a collection of goods that changed drastically in composition from year to year (all TV sets and no citrus one year, but lots of citrus and no TV sets the next), and which consisted at any given time of items that are themselves incomparable would be laughed out of court by most economists.

[7]Willard Van Orman Quine, *From a Logical Point of View* (Cambridge, Mass.: Harvard University Press, 1953), 129.

[8]For some leading references see Appendix I, below, and Louis Guttman, "An Outline of Some New Methodology of Social Research," *Public Opinion Quarterly* (1954-55): 395-404.

II.

There is really nothing mysterious or even very complicated about the Guttman scale. It is simply a test of whether a series of criteria can be so arranged as to result in cumulative divisions of the population under study.[9] Thus if a man from Mars wanted to compare New York City buildings in regard to their height but lacked any quantitative concepts (such as the earthman's meter or inch) he could still pick a series of buildings and use them to define a rank order of qualitative classes. He could, for example, classify all buildings on Manhattan as to whether they were at least as tall as the following named examples:

	As high as:			Not as high as:		
Building Classes	Empire State Building	Chrysler Building	Guggenheim Museum	Empire State Building	Chrysler Building	Guggenheim Museum
Type I	X	X	X			
Type II		X	X	X		
Type III			X	X	X	
Type IV				X	X	X

Now if our Martian visitor remained on Manhattan long enough he would discover that *all* of the thousands of buildings in the area fall exactly into one of the above four cumulative categories, and that nowhere—on earth or on Mars—is there a building that is not as high as the Guggenheim Museum, not as high as the Chrysler Building, but which is as high as the Empire State Building. Hence we have here a perfect cumulative Guttman-type scale based on a series of qualitative distinctions. The result is a ranking of buildings that are either "more" or "less" high than certain others, but without any connotations of cardinal measurement. Thus the

---

[9]Probably the most lucid introduction to scaling is Edward Suchman, "The Logic of Scale Construction," *Educational and Psychological Measurement* (1950): 79-93. For a more detailed explanation see Samuel A. Stouffer et al., *Measurement and Prediction* (Gloucester, Mass.: Peter Smith, 1950), especially Chapters 1, 2, 3, and 6.

differences in height between the Empire State and Chrysler Building are not the same as that between the Chrysler Building and the Guggenheim Museum.

Simple as this approach may seem, it was not until the decade of the 1940s that a procedure was worked out for systematically applying it to social science data (so much of which is not "quantitative" in the sense of being suitable for cardinal measurement). This was finally done by Louis Guttman, a social psychologist working in the War Department's attitude measurement project during World War II. Opinion researchers had long been aware that the specific wording of a question often has a very considerable effect on the proportion of positive responses. To obtain greater reliability a number of related questions might be asked to try and evoke varying degrees of agreement about what appeared to be a single broad topic. But this introduced the danger—as yet little recognized by users of legislative index numbers—that some of the questions might relate to some dimension or variable other than the one supposedly being studied.

Guttman's solution to this problem of determining the uni-dimensionality of a series of questions was simply to define a preliminary universe of questions that seemed to be directly related to the basic attitude, then submit a series of questions from this collection to a group of respondents. If the questions do constitute cumulative criteria relating to a single attitude dimension among the various respondents then the answers to the questions will divide the respondents into a series of strictly cumulative groups.[10] Now the problem of whether the questions do in some purely objective sense relate to a single dimension is not at stake, nor does even a perfectly cumulative pattern of responses prove that the questions are even in a subjective sense related to a single dimension. The cumulative pattern among respondents is a necessary but not sufficient condition for

---

[10]There is a basic difference between direct measurements carried out on a physical dimension and the necessarily indirect measurements of psychophysics. In the latter the researcher never operates directly in terms of observations of the dimension itself, but must depend upon the respondents' various judgments that are assumed to be indicative of the dimension. This distinction is rightly stressed by Bergmann and Spence in their excellent article on "The Logic of Psychophysical Measurement," note 5, *supra*.

establishing that the questions themselves are cumulative criteria along a single dimension.

The attitude dimension, be it noted, is purely a hypothetical construct, something that cannot be directly observed but only inferred as the basis for observed consistencies in overt behavior.[11] In those cases where the Senate takes a series of votes on differing percentage cuts in a given program, or on differing dollar amounts of appropriations for a given function, or on requiring a different number of senators to invoke cloture the result is generally a series of perfectly cumulative divisions. Of course, if this were the only value of scaling it would indeed be open to the oft-heard criticism of "proving the obvious." Fortunately, it turns out that many of the major areas of policy difference, such as labor-management relations, rent control, public housing, economic controls, foreign aid, reciprocal trade, and so forth often involve similar cumulative divisions of attitude along what appears to be a series of dimensions.

A very simple geometric metaphor will indicate the difference between a scaleable series of votes and the hodgepodge of measures often lumped together into numerical indexes. The oft-cited but little understood Arthur F. Bentley is the source of this suggestion—he wrote:

> If we take all the men of our society, say all the citizens of the United Stabs, and look upon them as a spherical mass, we can pass an unlimited number of planes through the center of the sphere each plane representing some principle of classification. . . . Assuming perhaps hundreds, perhaps thousands, of planes passed through the sphere, we get a great confusion of the groups. No one set of groups, that is no set distinguished on the basis of any one plane, will be an adequate grouping of the whole mass.[12]

It is this "great confusion of the groups" that intrigues those who study pressure groups. But it is the great merit of scale analysis that it orders this apparent confusion into sets of cumulative groups that can be distinguished

---

[11]For a suggestive diagram of the relation between overall ideology, less general attitudes, and specific opinions see H. J. Eysenck, *The Psychology of Politics* (London: Routledge and K. Paul, 1954), 112.

[12]Arthur Fisher Bentley, *The Process of Government* (Cambridge, Mass.: Belknap Press, 1967), 207.

along various dimensions. In doing so scaling provides the *sine qua non* for measurement.

Now if we let Bentley's sphere represent the total membership of the Senate and the planes represent the division on each roll call vote we find one of two types of situations. In Figure 1-A below the planes do not intersect, that is, there is no criss-crossing and hence the votes can be said to be criteria potentially relating to a single dimension (and thus defining a single variable). If, however, the result is a confusion of criss crossing, overlapping classifications—as in Figure 1-B below—then by no stretch of the imagination can they be said to relate to any single dimension.

At this point it may be well to turn from general discussion to examination of how a scale of legislative attitude may be constructed in actual practice. The 1949 Senate struggle over extension of rent control (involving HR 1731) is an example of a situation where scaling can be applied. Table 2 groups 94 of the then 96 senators (two of whom missed all or almost all of the votes) into 12 ordinal rankings that range from those most favorable to a "strong" rent control act to those most opposed. The rankings are based on the senators' stands on 11 roll call votes taken on passage of the bill or adoption of various proposed amendments. The following lists, in order of increasing strength for the procontrol position, the 11 issues, the sponsors of the amendments, the response scored as procontrol, and the margin of the roll call vote:

    1.   Senator Magnuson: Extend existing law for two years (Yea vote is scored as pro-control); defeated, 10-75.

    2.   Senator McClellan: Drop criminal penalties for willful violations (Nay is pro-control), adopted, 52-30.

    3.   Senator Bricker: Retain present system for eviction (Nay is pro-control); defeated, 42-44.

    4.   Senator Bricker: Allow a "reasonable return" on "reasonable value" of housing (Nay is procontrol); defeated, 34-47.

    5.   Senator Bricker: Motion to recommit conference report (Nay is pro-control); defeated, 33-53.

    6.   Senator Bricker: Decontrol hotels, motels trailers, and premises unrented from 1945-48 (Nay is pro-control); defeated, 29-53.

    7.   Senator Bricker: Limit extension of controls to September 30, 1949 (Nay is pro-control), defeated, 22-64.

Figure 1-A. *Cumulative Scale of Groupings Along a Single Dimension*

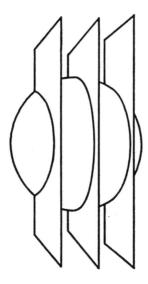

Figure 1-B. *A Confusion of Groups Based on Criteria from Several Different Dimensions*

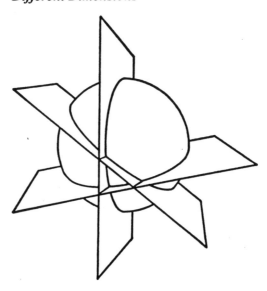

8. Senator Cordon: Require federal government to pay to landlords the difference between "reasonable rental value" and rent ceiling (Nay is procontrol); defeated, 20-59.

9. Senator Capehart: Provide for progressive decontrol, beginning with high cost rental units of September 30, 1949, extending on to include low cost units by June 30, 1950 (Nay is procontrol); defeated, 18-62.

10. Vote on passage of Senate version of bill providing for temporary extension but subject to local option in each state at the discretion of the state governor (Yea is pro-control); passed, 68-10.

11. Vote on adoption of conference committee version (Yea is procontrol); passed, 78-11.

In Table 2 procontrol responses are checked in the appropriate columns on the left-hand side of the center dividing line and anticontrol responses in columns on the right-hand side. The most procontrol senators are thus in the group at the top of the scale, and those progressively less procontrol are listed in subsequent groups ranging to the most anticontrol group at the bottom of the scale. The senators' individual stands on the 11 votes are taken from the 1949 *Congressional Quarterly*. Record votes are indicated by an "X" in the appropriately numbered column on the pro or anti side; pairs or announced stands are indicated by a diagonal: "/". Where a senator neither votes nor indicated his stand a zero is entered in *both* the procontrol and anticontrol columns for that issue.

Of the 1,034 senatorial responses indicated in the scale in Table 2 all but 29 fall within the perfect scale patterns (41 responses are unknown and are scored neither for nor against the consistency of the scale pattern). Thus if we were to try to reproduce each senator's complete voting record on these 11 issues knowing only his rank position on this scale (and his missed votes) we would be correct 97.1 percent of the time (that is, on all but 29 of the 1,034 responses). Guttman has christened this percentage the "coefficient of reproducibility" and uses it as a basic test of the extent to which a series of items may be said to relate to a single dimension. For a perfect cumulative pattern the figure is 100.0 percent. At the opposite extreme, even random guesses as to dichotomous responses should result in about 50 percent reproducibility. Although several alternative scoring formulas have been suggested, a discussion of their respective merits would lead us too far afield. Provided that the responses to most items are not too lop-sided (e.g., votes of 90 to 3) and that the nonscale responses are not too heavily concentrated on a single issue, a coefficient of reproducibility of at least 90

Table 2. Scale Analysis of Eleven Votes on Rent Control in the Senate in 1949

Senators	Party	Procontrol											Anticontrol										
		1	2	3	4	5	6	7	8	9	10	11	1	2	3	4	5	6	7	8	9	10	11
Pepper	D	X	X	X	X	X	X	X	X	X	X	X											
Taylor	D	X	X	X	X	X	X	X	X	X	X	X											
Humphrey	D	X	X	X	X	X	X	X	X	X	X	X											
Murray	D	X	X	X	/	X	X	X	X	X	/	X											
Chavez	D	X	O	X	/	/	X	X	/	X	/	X		O									
Myers	D	X	X	X	X	X	X	X	X	X	X	X											
Magnuson	D	X	X	X	X	X	X	X	X	X	X	X											
Kilgore	D	X	X	X	X	X	X	X	X	X	X	X											
Neely	D	X	X	X	X	X	X	X	X	X	X	X											
Hunt	D	X	X	X	X	X	X	X	X	X	X	X											
Hill	D		X	X	X	X	X	X	X	X	X	X	X										
Sparkman	D		X	X	X	X	X	X	X	X	X	X	X										
Hayden	D		X	X	X	X	X	X	X	X	X	X	X										
McMahon	D		X	X	X	X	X	X	X	X	X	X	X										
Frear	D		X	X	X	X	/	X	X	O	X	X	O										
Miller	D	O	O	X	O	X	X	O	O	O	/	X	O	O		O			O	O	O	O	
Douglas	D	X	X	X	X	X	X	X	X	X	X	X	X										
Lucas	D	X	X	X	X	X	X	X	X	X	X	X	X										

Senator	Party	Votes
Lodge	R	X · / · X X X X X X X X —
Anderson	D	X · X X X X X X X X X O
Ives	R	X · X X X X X X X X X X
Wagner	D	O · / / / / / / / / /
Langer	R	O · X X X X X X X X X
Kerr	D	X · X X X X X X X X X X
Morse	R	X · X X X X X X X X
Green	D	X · X X X X X X X X X
McGrath	D	O O O · X X X X X X X X
Maybank	D	O O O · X X X X X X X X
Kefauver	D	X X X X X X X X X X O
Johnson (Tex.)	D	X X X X X X X O O O
Thomas (Utah)	D	X X X X X X X X X X
Aiken	R	X X X X X X X X X X
Flanders	R	X O X / / / / / X X X
Thomas (Okla.)	D	O O O X X X X X X O O
Fulbright	D	X X X X X X X X X X
Downey	D	X X X X X X X X X X
Gillette	D	X X X X X X X X X X
Chapman	D	X X X X X X X X X X
Withers	D	X X X X X X X X X X
Ellender	D	X X X X X X X X X X
Long	D	X X X X O O O X X X
Stennis	D	X X X X X X X X X X
Johnston	D	X X X X X X X X X X
McKellar	D	X X X X X X X X X X

Table 2. *Continued*

Senators	Party	Procontrol											Anticontrol										
		1	2	3	4	5	6	7	8	9	10	11	1	2	3	4	5	6	7	8	9	10	11
Connally	D			X		X	X	X	X	X	X	X	X	X		X							
Robertson	D			X	X	X	X	X	X	O	X	X	X	X	X						O		
O'Mahoney	D			X	X	X	X	X	X	X	X	X	X	X	X								
McCarran	D			X		X	X	X	X	X	X	X	X	X	X	X							
McFarland	D				X	X	X	X	X	X	X	X	X	X	X								
Johnson (Colo.)	D				X	X	X	X	X	X	X	X	X	X	X								
Holland	D				X	X	X	X	X	X	X	X	X	X	X								
Smith (Me.)	R				X	X	X	X	X	X	X	X	X	X	X								
Tobey	R		X		X	X		X	X		X	X	X		X		X		X				
Smith (N.J.)	R				/	/		/	/	/	/	X	/	/	/				/				
Hoey	D				X	X	X	X	X	X	X	X	X	X	X								
George	D					X	X	X	X	X	X	X	X	X	X	X							
O'Conor	D					X	X	X	X	X	X	X	X	X	X	X							
Tydings	D					X	X	X	O	X	/	X	X	X	/	/				O			
Russell	D		O	/			X	X	X	O	X	X	X	O	X	X	/				O		
Thye	R		/	/			X	/	/	/	/	X	/			X	X						

176

	Party																				
Knowland	R	X		O		X	X	X	X	X	X		O	/	X	O	X			O	
Baldwin	R								O	X	X		X	X	X	X	X	X			
Brewster	R			O		X	X	X	X	X	X		X	O	X	X	X	X		O	
Saltonstall	R				O	X	X	X	X	X	X		X	/	X	O	O	X		X	
Vandenberg	R			X	X	X	X	X	X	X	X		X	X	X	X	X	X			
Hendrickson	R					X	X	X	X	X	X		X	X	X	X	X	X			
McCarthy	R			X		X	X	X	X	X	X		X	X	X	X	X	X			
McClellan	D		X		X	X	X	X	X	X	X		X	X	X	X	X	X		X	
Donnell	R				X	X	X	X	X	X	X		X	X	X	X	X	X			
Martin	R			X	X	X	X	X	X	X	X		X	X	X	X	X				
Watkins	R			X	X	X	X	X	X	X	X		X	X	X	X	X		X		
Byrd	D			O	X	O	X	X	X	X	X		X	/	X	O		O			X
Wiley	R			O	X	X	X	X	X	X	X		X	X	X	X	O	X			
Milliken	R			X	X	X	X	X	X	X	X		X	X	X	X			X		
Hickenlooper	R			X	X	X	X	X	X	X	X		X	X	X	X	O	O		O	O
Reed	R			O	X	O	X	O	X	O	O		X	X	O	X	X	O		O	O
Schoeppel	R			O	X	X	X	X	X	X	X		X	X	X	X					
Ferguson	R			X	X	O	X	X	X	X	X		X	X	X	X					
Malone	R			X	X	X	X	X	X	X	X		X	X	X	X		O			
Bridges	R			X	/	/	X	/	X	/	X		X	/	X	/	X				
Taft	R			X	/	/	X	X	X	X	X		X	/	X	X	X				
Williams	R			X	X	X	X	X	X	X	X		X	X	X	X		X			
Kem	R	X	X	X	X	X	X	X	X	X	X		X	X	X	X					

177

Table 2. *Continued*

Senators	Party	Procontrol											Anticontrol										
		1	2	3	4	5	6	7	8	9	10	11	1	2	3	4	5	6	7	8	9	10	11
Capehart	R				O							O	X	X	X	X	O	X	X	X	X	/	O
Jenner	R												X	X	X	X	X	X	X	/	X	/	X
Ecton	R												X	X	X	X	X	X	X	X	X	X	X
Wherry	R												X	X	X	X	X	X	X	X	X	X	X
Butler	R												X	X	X	/	/	X	X	X	X	X	/
Cordon	R												X	X	O	/	X	X	X	X	X	X	X
Mundt	R								X				X	X	X	X	X	X	X	X	X	X	X
Cain	R									X			/	/	/	/	/	/	/	/		/	/
Gurney	R									X			X	X	X	X	X	X	X	X		X	X
Bricker	R							X		X			X	X	X	X	X	X	X	X	X	X	X
Young	R							X		X			X	X	X	X	X	X	X	X	X	X	X

Senators omitted because of number of unrecorded stands: Eastland D; Graham D.

178

or preferably 95 percent may be regarded as the minimum for an acceptable scale.

Now with 11 votes there are 2,048 possible combinations of positive or negative responses (equal to 2n where n = number of votes involved). But there are only 12 (that is, $n + 1$, where n is number of votes) perfect scale patterns. In Table 2 no less than 72 of the 94 senators fall into one of these 12 perfect scale patterns. Thus over 70 percent of the individuals classified fall within the predicted response patterns although these patterns are less than one percent of the total possible patterns.

The remaining nonscale response types (the 22 senators *not* fitting one of the 12 perfect scale patterns) must be assigned to one of the perfect patterns if they are to be included in the ranking. This has been done by assigning each to that scale pattern which he most closely approximates. Thus Senator Fulbright, for example, is assigned to rank III, from which he differs in his response on issue 8. If he were assigned to any other pattern, however, he would differ on more than one response (thus if he were assigned to rank XII, the bottom one he would differ on eight of the 11 issues).

Further details of scaling methodology could be pursued at some length, but for the purposes of this paper we want also to examine what sorts of questions can be explored by use of the scaling technique. What, for example, does the scale in Table 2 indicate about differences between the parties, or about differences between southern and nonsouthern Democrats? For greater convenience in handling this type question the 12 scale ranks—some of which are quite small—have been telescoped into four composite categories. The particular cut-off points are such that we cannot include exactly one-fourth of the senators in each composite grouping, but I have sought to approximate this figure so that the composites represent rough "quartiles." In terms of party the breakdown of the composite scale rankings is as follows:

Scale Categories

	I-II	III-IV	V-IX	X-XII	Total
# Reps.	6	3	11	22	42
# Dems.	28	18	6	0	52 (2 omitted)

Within the Democratic party the southern and nonsouthern senators compare on the *same* basis as follows:

#S. Dems.	6	10	4	0	20	(2 omitted)
#non-S. Dems.	22	8	2	0	32	

In this particular scale ranking the difference between southern and nonsouthern Democratic senators is not as striking as that between members of the major parties. Now at this point we can turn from the problem of ranking attitudes along a hypothetical dimension to the closely related question of "who votes with whom."

In approaching this problem Stuart Rice, and later Hermann Beyle, suggested that the number of times each possible pair of legislators voted together on the prevailing side on a series of issues be counted. These dyadic relations should then be entered in a square table large enough to list every legislator across the top of the page and down the side. Beyle suggests the names then be arranged, as nearly as possible, in such an order that those agreeing most often are in the upper-left corner. In the perfect case the number of agreements, on the prevailing side of each issue, between this bloc and the other legislators shades off gradually down to those at the bottom-right corner of the page, who voted opposite the majority bloc on every issue.[13]

This technique, generally known as attribute-cluster-bloc analysis, is obviously closely related to scale analysis. The difficulty with it, other than that it requires almost double the amount of clerical work necessary if one defines a dimension, is that on the prevailing side it is absolutely limited to cases where one block includes at least one-half of the total membership (a fairly rare occurrence). This is obvious since in a perfect bloc arrangement the prevailing block can "prevail" only if it includes at least one-half of the membership. In practice smaller blocs may seem to exist, but only due to the affects of absences or of irregularities in the pattern. In the cases of other than perfectly cumulative blocs the assignment of individuals who do not exactly "fit" the bloc pattern is exactly analogous to the assigning of nonscale types within a scale pattern. In cases of missed votes, however,

---

[13]See Hermann C. Beyle, *Identification and Analysis of Attribute-Cluster-Blocs* (Chicago: The University of Chicago Press, 1931).

bloc analysis automatically lowers the absent legislator's total number of agreements, and hence his classification whereas scaling provides a rationale for assigning him in accord with the way we would expect him to have voted had he followed the scale pattern.

The attribute-cluster-bloc approach thus compares the records of each possible pairing of legislators, whereas scaling compares each legislator's record against the perfect scale pattern. Now as a matter of logic—a subject that I feel has been unduly neglected by political scientists—if the records of two individuals are related to a given standard in a known manner it should be possible to deduce from this how they are related to each other. If this can be done then scaling has not just one but *two* possible interpretations: not only as a technique for ordinal measurement of legislative attitudes, but as a means for showing the existence of legislative blocs.

Now in a perfect scale we know, without performing any sort of cluster analysis, that each individual in each given scale type voted with all other individuals in the same type on *every* issue considered. We know, further, that all the individuals in a given scale type voted identically as all the individuals in an adjoining scale type (above or below them) *except on one* issue, and we know which issue this is (something not evident from a cluster-bloc analysis). In fact, the scale pattern tells us how many times individuals in *any* given scale type voted together with the individuals in *any other* type, and on which issues they agreed and on which they differed. The two extreme scale types, for example, vote opposite on *all* of the issues in the scale.

Every perfect scale pattern thus constitutes, by definition, a perfect attribute-cluster-bloc analysis, and vice-versa. The only difference is that to properly bring out the cluster-blocs it is necessary to arrange the legislators so that the maximum numbers (of agreements between pairs of legislators) are concentrated, as in matrix algebra, along the main diagonal rather than in a corner. The lesser values then shade off symmetrically to both sides of the diagonal, reaching zero in the upper-right and lower-left corners (thus indicating the total disagreement existing between the extreme scale types). Had Professor Beyle only arranged his data in this form he should have arrived at the basic concept of a cumulative scale a full 25 years ahead of the sociologists!

Although a cluster-bloc analysis of voting on the Rent Control Act would not add to what is already evident in Table 2, it does suggest the possibility of using scaling to carry out a *two-dimensional* cluster-bloc analysis. That is, prepare a cross-tabulation with as many horizontal rows as there are different scale rankings on one scale and as many vertical columns as there are rankings on a second scale. Then each legislator can be entered in the unique cell that identifies his voting pattern on both dimensions. Assuming that both scales are perfect then all senators in a given row will have voted identically on all issues included in Scale 1, all senators in a given column will have voted identically on all issues in Scale 2, and thus all senators in a given cell of the table will have voted identically on all issues in both scales. In such a cross-tabulation the extent of voting agreement or disagreement between any individual legislators or groups of legislators in regard to two different dimensions is evident at a glance.

Such a two-dimensional analysis of Senate voting is summarized in Table 3, below. Rankings on the labor-management relations scale are indicated along the horizontal axis (with Rank I on the left as the most prolabor) and rankings on the previously presented rent control scale are indicated along the vertical axis (with Rank I at the top as the procontrol position). Space limitations preclude listing the individual senators in each cell of the tabulation, but it is interesting to note that all 10 senators in the upper right-hand corner of the table (indicated by an asterisk) are southern Democrats. These are the senators taking a relatively favorable stand on rent control, but maintaining a disapproving attitude toward organized labor. Conversely, in the lower left-hand corner (thus representing the reverse combination of views) is Senator Malone of Nevada. Although Malone generally represented a point of view somewhat to the right of Senator Goldwater, Nevada is a small state where the mining unions are of considerable political importance. Thus in 1947 Malone voted against passage of the Taft Hartley Act and to uphold President Truman's veto of it.

Although support for the "liberal" position of labor relations and rent control is obviously correlated, Table 3 indicates the advantages for analysis in treating these as separate policy dimensions. If all the votes on both scales were included in a single numerical index, for example, the result would be a very poor guide to the actual distribution of attitudes. Thus Senator Malone, the senators holding a middle view on both issues, and the southern Democrats in the upper-right of the table would be likely to have quite similar scores on the combined index.

Table 3. *Comparison of Senators' Rankings on Labor Relations and Rent Control Dimensions, 1949*

Position in Rent Control Ranks	Number of Senators — Position in Labor Relations Ranks									
	I	II	III	IV	V	VI	VII	VIII	Unk.	Total
I	8	1	1							10
II	5	8	4	3	1	1		2*		24
III		3	5			2		4*		14
IV		2	1		1	1		2*		7
V-VI				1	2			2*		5
VII						3	4			7
VII-IX							3	2		5
X				1**		1	4	3		9
XI-XII		1				1	3	8		13
Unknown								1	1	2
Total	13	15	11	5	4	9	14	24	1	96

*Category composed solely of southern Democrats.
**Senator Malone of Nevada.

Where the same policy dimension comes up for debate and is voted on in different sessions of Congress the same simple cross-tabulation procedure can be used to trace shifts in attitude over time. These permit analysis of the impact of change of party control of the presidency. Where the same subject comes up for a number of years, as with foreign aid, the analysis can be carried out in terms of a panel study. But rather than explore these problems here it may be wise to conclude with a more detailed application of the basic scaling technique to some selected problems of party and sectional divergences in the Senate in the period from 1949-1956.

III.

After this rather long excursion into problems of method we turn more directly to the theme of internal party differences in the Senate. For the period 1949 through 1956 a total of 56 acceptable scales of Senate voting patterns were constructed. These scales cover most, though by no means all, of the major controversial issues of the period on which there were a number of roll call votes. For each scale a breakdown by major party was prepared, and then intraparty breakdowns were run to compare southern and nonsouthern Democrats (taking the 11 ex-Confederate states as "the South"), as well as northeastern Republicans (from states north of the Potomac and east of Ohio) and other Republicans. Rather than treat each scale separately, as a research nominalist might, or try to cover all 56 by a single description, as a Neoplatonist might, I have sought to group the scales into a few conceptual categories based on differences in relative extent of party cohesion.

The first of my four categories is one designed to indicate scale areas of relatively "high" cohesion, and hence relatively sharp party difference. This pattern, which approaches the ideal of the "responsible parties" proponents, may be the result of a situation where constituency interests largely parallel party divisions, or of a strictly partisan party issue, or of extraordinarily successful maneuvering by the party leadership. The defining characteristic for this category is that there be a cut-off point in the scale ranking such that at least 80 percent of the Democrats will be on one side and at least 80 percent of the Republicans on the other. This pattern can perhaps be made somewhat clearer by a simple figure in which the successive scale rankings on the subject are indicated on the horizontal axis—for greater simplicity I have combined the rankings into four of as

Figure 2. *Party Profile in Area of "Relatively Sharp"*
Party Differences

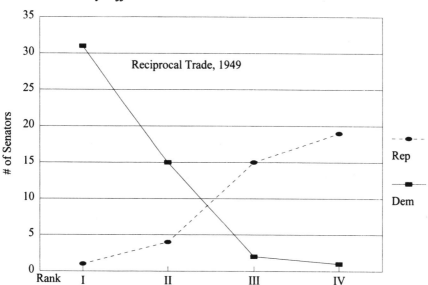

nearly equal size as possible, with the more "liberal-internationalist"
position on the left. The *number* of senators in each ranking is indicated,
separately by party, on the vertical axis. Figure 2 presents the party profile
in a typical Type I case: the Reciprocal Trade Act Extension scale for 1949.

Now in scale dimensions in which the parties as a whole differ as
sharply as this, intraparty sectional differences are obviously at a minimum.
Where almost all Democrats oppose almost all Republicans there can be no
basic distinction between southern and nonsouthern Democrats. But how
often is the difference between the parties this sharp? Of the 56 scales used
in this study 15 fall within the category of relatively sharp party disagreement (as defined above). These 15 scale areas and the year in which they
occurred are as follows:

Reciprocal Trade Act Extension, 1949
Confirmation of "Liberal" Appointees, 1949
Cut Funds for Army Engineers, 1949
Economic Controls (Defense Production Act), 1950
Universal Military Training, 1951

185

Increase Postal Rates, 1951
Extend Rent Control, 1952
Cut Funds for Army Engineers, 1952
Cut Funds for Federal Road Aid, 1952
Economic Controls (Defense Production Act), 1953
Rubber Plant Disposal, 1953
Amend Atomic Energy Act, 1954
Amend Revenue Code, 1954
Control of Subversion, 1954
Postal Pay Increase, 1955

In 21 of the remaining scale areas there is a cut-off point such that at least two-thirds of the Democrats are on one side and at least two-thirds of the Republicans on the other, but in which one or both parties fail to meet the more strict requirement set for category I. These 21 dimensions have been designated as policy areas of "moderate" party difference. Figure 3, showing the distribution by party on the 1951 foreign aid scale, illustrates the increased overlap of attitudes found in these scales. Although the differences between the parties are still quite noticeable, sectional intraparty breakdowns also begin to reveal some interesting differences. On this particular scale, for example, the distribution of southern and nonsouthern Democratic senators is as follows:

	(Lib.)			(Cons.)		
	Rank I	II	III	IV	Unknown	Total
#S. Dems.	6	6	7	3	0	22
# non-S. Dems.	18	4	3	0	3	28

The two more "liberal" categories of this scale ranking thus include 22 of the 25 classified nonsouthern Democrats but only 12 of the 22 southerners.

Although it might be of some interest to analyze the extent of sectional differences in all the Category II scales, it seems preferable to concentrate our analysis on the remaining 20 scale areas of "low" party cohesion. In these cases, where one or both parties are so badly split as to be unable to muster even a two-to-one majority on either half of the scale, some variable other than party is obviously exerting powerful influence. The graphic patterns for the scale areas of low cohesion are extremely varied, in fact, so much so that I have subdivided them into two general categories. The first and by far most frequent is what I have termed the ordinary pattern of low

Figure 3. *Party Profile in Area of "Moderate"*
Party Difference

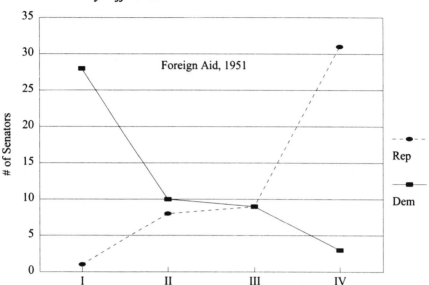

cohesion. This includes those cases where the parties are still at least somewhat skewed in opposite directions or are almost identically distributed. There is, however, a very striking pattern that occasionally develops in which one party will predominate at the two polar extremes (thus presenting a bimodal distribution) while the other party is concentrated in the middle two categories of the scale (thus resembling a normal curve). Because of its explosive implications for internal party adjustment I have regarded this rather rare situation as worthy of a separate classification of its own.

The difference between the "ordinary" pattern of low cohesion and the "bimodal" pattern can be seen by comparing the foreign aid scales of 1953 and 1954. In the former year, shown in Figure 4, the two parties were rather similarly spread through all four classifications (those in Rank I were the strongest supporters, those in Rank IV the strongest opponents). This was a temporary phenomenon resulting from somewhat decreased Democratic support for the aid program under a Republican administration and an even more noticeable increase in Republican senatorial support for the program. By 1954, an election year in which Eisenhower stressed his concern for the

Figure 4. *Party Profile in Area of "Slight" Party Difference, with "Ordinary" Distribution*

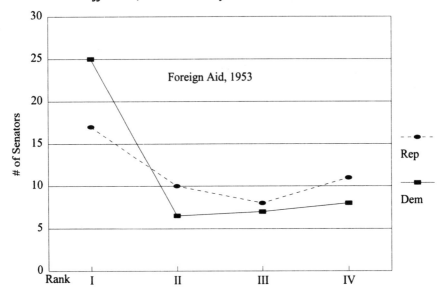

Figure 5. *Party Profile in Area of "Slight" Party Difference, with "Bimodal" Distribution of Republicans*

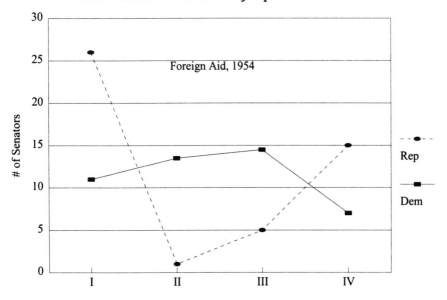

foreign aid program, the situation had changed to that indicated in Figure 5. The Republicans by 1954 were by and large to be found either among the most enthusiastic supporters or among the most bitter opponents of the aid program. The Democrats, however, were concentrated largely in the middle categories. Comparison of Figures 3, 4, and 5 dramatically illustrates the changing party line-up on the question of foreign aid.

The bimodal pattern occurs for the Republicans on the foreign aid scales of 1954 and 1956. For the Democrats the 1949 cloture rule fight presents the clearest bimodal pattern although the Displaced Persons Act of 1950 also meets the minimum requirements for inclusion. Senate Democrats also closely approached the bimodal pattern in the 1949 labor relations scale (see Table 3) and 1950 Revenue Act scale. In all six of these scales including the last two marginal cases, the bimodal pattern occurs in the ranks of the party in control of the White House. In each instance sectional cleavages within the bimodally divided party are quite pronounced. One might conclude that the political necessities involved in winning the presidency (as in the case of civil rights and the Democrats) or of carrying out absolutely necessary national policy (as in the case of foreign aid under the Republicans) require the party in power to push programs that threaten to split the party along sectional lines in the Senate.

Of the 20 scales of relatively slight party difference there are 11 in which both parties are sharply divided. In four additional scales only the Democrats are so split, and in five additional ones only the Republicans are so split. Table 4, below presents the customary four-rank breakdown between southern and nonsouthern Democrats on the 15 scales in which the Democrats as a whole were sharply divided. The scales are arranged in a rough order to indicate the decreasing importance of the sectional division as a possible explanation for the party disarray. Thus the first-listed scale, involving the 1949 attempt to modify the Senate's cloture rule and thus facilitate passage of FEPC legislation, presents an extremely sharp division. On the other hand, the last listed scale, on continuing aid to Tito in 1956, indicates almost identical divisions within the southern and nonsouthern Democratic ranks. On most of the scales, however, there is a fairly clear difference between what might be termed the center of gravity among the southern Democrats as compared to that of the nonsouthern Democrats.

From this extremely brief summary of some aspects of one possible application of scale analysis one can draw additional evidence for a number of familiar generalizations. A detailed examination of all 56 scales leaves

Table 4. *Comparison of Southern and Nonsouthern Democrats'*
Rankings in Fifteen Scale Areas of Low Party Cohesion in
Senate Voting, 1949-1956

Scale Subject and year	Type Democrat	Number of Senators in Each "Quartile" Rank				Total Classified
		I	II	III	IV	
Change Cloture Rule	S	1	1	0	19	21
(FEPC), 1949	non-S	17	4	6	5	32
Electoral College	S	1	1	1	18	21
"Reform," 1956	non-S	14	4	3	6	27
Economic Controls	S	3	3	13	0	19
(DPA), 1951	non-S	15	8	1	1	25
Displaced Persons	S	6	1	6	7	20
Act, 1950	non-S	24	3	0	2	29
Reorganize Regulatory	S	3	4	10	3	20
Commissions, 1950	non-S	17	4	3	2	26
Foreign Aid,	S	3	3	11	3	20
1954	non-S	7	11	3	3	24
Excise Tax Cuts,	S	4	6	7	4	21
1954	non-S	17	4	4	1	26
Foreign Aid,	S	7	4	6	4	21
1955	non-S	18	6	3	0	27
Use of Treaty	S	7	3	4	4	18
Power, 1953	non-S	16	3	3	2	24
Foreign Aid,	S	9	3	4	6	22
1953	non-S	15	4	3	2	24
Revenue Act,	S	4	7	1	10	22
1951	non-S	16	5	3	3	27
Revenue Act,	S	6	4	4	6	20
1950	non-S	14	4	0	7	25
Natural Gas Act,	S	4	5	0	13	22
1956	non-S	15	2	2	8	27
Foreign Aid,	S	5	5	7	5	22
1956	non-S	14	4	5	4	27
Continue Aid to	S	8	2	5	7	22
Tito, 1956	non-S	10	3	3	10	26

one with the impression that in most of these attitude areas the centers of gravity of the two major parties differed significantly. In almost one-third of the areas the division between the parties was quite sharp, although in another one-third the differences between them must be regarded as rather slight. Very low cohesion within one party was generally accompanied by low cohesion within the other, although in a few crucial areas one party would be bimodally split while the other party was massed in a moderate position between the opposing wings of the former party.

To speak of "the" southern Democrats as a monolithic bloc voting the same way on most issues during this period would be to make a very serious error of analysis. On only two of the 56 scales (1949 cloture fight and 1956 electoral college reform) did the southern Democrats even approach unanimity (and even here Pepper and Kefauver deviated on the former and Long, Gore, and Ellender deviated—with Kefauver absent campaigning—on the latter).[14]

On a considerable number of scales, however, the center of gravity of the southern Democrats is obviously more to the conservative and—in recent years—isolationist end of the policy spectrum. That is, both southern and nonsouthern Democrats are split within their own ranks, but two out-of three southerners support the "conservative-isolationist" view on labor-management policy, displaced persons, taxation and revenue policy, use of the treaty power, public housing, rent control, and some other economic issues, while two out of three nonsouthern Democrats will support the "liberal-internationalist" viewpoint. And there still remain a good many areas in which the two sectional wings of the Democratic party are more or less united in opposition to the Republicans or in which both wings are about equally split.

Thus we reach the melancholy conclusion that the difference in Senate voting patterns between southern and nonsouthern Democrats is a complex matter of many varying shades of gray, plus occasional spots of black and white. It would be misleading to describe the general situation in terms of

---

[14]Scale analysis thus generally confirms for the 1949-1956 period most of the conclusions reached by Professor Key in his analysis of individual roll call votes of the 1933-45 period in Chapter 16 of *Southern Politics*. Scaling, however, may make it easier to distinguish instances of a differing center of gravity even in those situations where there is no sharp dividing line between the sections.

some selected instance of black and white contrast, or of total lack of difference between the two. On the other hand, it seems to me of very slight value to attempt to reduce the situation to some hypothetical "average" situation (which may not correspond to a single real instance) without paying any attention to the very considerable dispersion around this central tendency. If we are to be very accurate I think such a complex situation requires at least a relatively complex description.

For many purposes scale analysis does afford an important new technique for providing more accurate descriptions of many aspects of legislative *voting* behavior. This, of course, may not throw much light upon the broad range of questions involved in a detailed legislative case study. Scaling points up the need for more careful definitions of the variables we seek to measure, as well as the necessity for a more cautious approach to the problems of cardinal measurement.[15] Scaling affords visible proof of the serious methodological weakness of most current indexes of legislative attitudes. It also suggests the importance of developing relational statistics, such as our ordinal rankings, which indicate structure without attempting to establish a strict quantitative metric.[16] Scaling also constitutes an important improvement on existing techniques, such as attribute-cluster-bloc analysis, for the study of who votes with whom.

Scaling, in common with other formal disciplines such as mathematics and symbolic logic, seeks to make more obvious the relationships holding between a large number of factors. As with these other disciplines absolutely nothing is added to the significance of the original data. But to admit that nothing is added to what was already implicit in the data is not

---

[15]As Herbert A. Simon has aptly observed, "most of the arguments against 'quantitizing' or 'measuring' the 'qualitative' variables encountered in the social sciences *stem from ignorance* of how flexible the concept 'quantity' is, and how indefinite the lines between quantity and quality." Simon, "Notes on the Observation and Measurement of Political Power," *Journal of Politics* (1953): 506-16, at 513 (italics mine).

[16]The core of mathematics is *not* number, as has sometimes been said, but a concern for order of structure. James R. Newman's excellent four-volume study of *The World of Mathematics* makes this, and many other important points quite clear in terms that even a nonmathematician can appreciate. It may be that political scientists should concern themselves a bit less with the gadgetry of applied statistics, and a bit more with the elements of symbolic logic and pure mathematics.

to say that we—the harrassed and imperfect observers—do not see relationships that we could not have grasped from merely observing the original data. What is there and what we know about what is there are quite different matters at the methodological level as much as they are at the epistemological level.

Like mathematics and logic, scaling can tell the omniscient mind absolutely nothing new. The results of such tautological processes are already present, in somewhat less obvious form, in the raw data. If God exists and is omniscient, then He knows all possible deductions, correlations, scale patterns, and all other possible relationships without having to perform any calculations. Hence, as has often been remarked, those who feel on a par with the Deity have no need for logic or mathematics. Those of us with lesser endowments continue to find a considerable advantage in the use of such formal techniques.

Despite its many advantages scaling is by no means a research panacea. It requires a volume of data that is often unattainable. And even given the data, scale analysis can only be useful for handling certain types of questions and not others. Thus, perhaps the most important question of legislative voting analysis—why so-and-so votes a given way—is almost completely beyond its range. The advent of the steel plow has not entirely replaced the earlier wooden version, nor has it yet made the desert or the arctic bloom. Political scientists who, like Voltaire, seek to cultivate their gardens, may find the simpler research techniques satisfactory for some purposes. For many other purposes I think scaling offers very important advantages. And for many yet different purposes I fear we must continue the search for still other new and more powerful research tools.

APPENDIX I

A Selective
Bibliography
of Scale Analysis

1. **Basic Explanation of Guttman Scale Technique:**

   Louis Guttman, "A Basis for Scaling Qualitative Data," *American Sociological Review* (April 1944): 139-50.

   Samuel A. Stouffer, Louis Guttman, et al. *Measurement and Prediction* (Princeton, N.J.: Princeton University Press, 1950), especially pages 3-19 and 60-90.

   Edward A. Suchman, "The Logic of Scale Construction," *Educational and Psychological Measurement* (Spring 1950): 79-93.

2. **Further Developments in Scaling Technique:**

   Samuel A. Stouffer et al., "A Technique for Improving Cumulative Scale," *Public Opinion Quarterly* (Summer 1952): 273-91, reprinted as Ch. 17 in M. W. Riley et al., *Sociological Studies in Scale Analysis* (New Brunswick, N.J.: Rutgers University Press, 1954).

   Louis Guttman, "The Israel Alpha Technique for Scale Analysis," in M. W. Riley et al., *op. cit.,* 410-15.

   Louis Guttman, "An Outline of Some New Methodology for Social Research," *Public Opinion Quarterly* (1954-55): 395-404.

   Paul F. Lazarsfeld (ed.), *Mathematical Thinking in the Social Sciences* (Glencoe, Ill.: Free Press, 1954), especially Ch. 5 (by Guttman) and Ch. 7 (by Lazarsfeld).

3. **Logical Importance of Cumulative Scales:**

   Carl G. Hempel, *Fundamentals of Concept Formation in Empirical Science,* International Encyclopedia of Unified Science, Vol. II, No. 7 (1952), especially pages 39-69.

   Gustav Bergmann and Kenneth W. Spence, "The Logic of Psychophysical Measurement," *Psychological Review* (1944), reprinted in H. Feigl and M. Brodbeck, *Readings in the Philosophy of Science* (New York: Appleton-Century-Crofts, 1953), pages 103-19 (especially 106-108).

4. Some Selected Applications of Scaling (including nonattitude data):

Samuel A. Stouffer et al., *The American Soldier,* Vols. I and II (New York: Science Eds., 1949) (data is processed by methods explained in *Measurement and Prediction*).

Samuel A. Stouffer, *Communism, Conformity and Civil Liberties* (Garden City, N.Y.: Doubleday, 1955) (see Appendix) pages 262-69 for use of "H-technique" or "contrived" composite items.

Margaret J. Hagood and Daniel O. Price, *Statistics for Sociologists* (New York: Holt, 1952 revised ed.), pp. 145-52 and 152-54.

Normal E. Green, "Scale Analysis of Urban Structures," *American Sociological Review* (February 1946): 8-13.

Herman M. Case, "Guttman Scaling Applied to Centers' Conservatism-Radicalism Battery," *American Journal of Sociology* (May 1953).

IV. Research and Publications of H. Douglas Price

BIBLIOGRAPHY

Research and Publications

"The Negro and Florida Politics, 1944-1952." 1953. M.A. thesis.

"Municipal Tort Liability: A Continuing Enigma." 1953. *University of Florida Law Review* 6 (Fall): 330-54 (with J. Allen Smith).

"Picketing—A Legal Cinderella." 1954. *University of Florida Law Review* 7 (Summer): 143-77.

"The Negro and Florida Politics, 1944-1954." 1955. *Journal of Politics* 17: 198-220.

"America's Newest Voter: A Florida Case Study." 1954-55. *Antioch Review* (Winter): 441-57 (with William G. Carleton).

"Massachusetts Campaign Finance in 1952." 1955. *Public Policy* 5:25-41.

"Negro Registration" (pp. 316-35) and "Are Southern Democrats Different? Scale Analysis of Senate Voting Patterns" (pp. 740-56). 1963. In *Politics and Social Life: An Introduction to Political Behavior*, ed. Nelson W. Polsby, Robert A Dentler, and Paul A. Smith. Boston: Houghton Mifflin.

The Negro and Southern Politics: A Chapter of Florida History. 1957. New York: New York University Press.

"Scale Analysis of Senate Voting Patterns, 1949-1956." 1958. Ph.D. dissertation.

Florida Voter's Guide. 1958. Gainesville: University of Florida (with Bruce Mason).

"Organizations: A Social Scientists View." 1959. Review article in *Public Administration Review* (Spring): 126-27.

"Scale Positions and 'Power' in the Senate." 1959. Comment on a paper by Robert Dahl. *Behavioral Science* 4:212-18 (co-authored with Duncan MacRae, Jr.).

The Metropolis and Its Problems: A Report Occasioned by the First Syracuse Seminar on Metropolitan Research. 1960. Syracuse: Syracuse University Press (with Roscoe Martin).

"How the American Voter Makes Up is Mind." 1960. *American Review* 1 (Autumn). Published by Johns Hopkins Bologna Center, Italy.

"Race, Religion and the Rules Committee: The Kennedy Aid-to-Education Bills." 1962. In *The Uses of Power: 7 Cases in American Politics,* ed. Alan F. Westin. New York: Harcourt, Brace, and World, Inc.

"Politics and the 'Pork Choppers'." 1962. In *The Politics of Reapportionment,* ed. Malcolm E. Jewell. New York: Atherton Press.

"Review of Robert A. Dahl's 'Who Governs?'" 1962. *Yale Law Journal* (July): 1589-96.

"Theories of the Public Interest." 1962. In *Politics and Public Affairs*, ed. Lynton Keith Caldwell. Bloomington, Ind.: Indiana University Press, 141-59.

Readings in Political Parties and Pressure Groups. 1964. New York: Crowell (with Frank J. Munger).

Conducted sample survey of Newburyport, Mass. ("Yankee City") in summer of 1964, and of Muncie, Indiana ("Middletown") in summer of 1965. Unpublished manuscript compares how cities have changed since studies by Warner and by the Lynds.

"The Congressional Career—Then and Now." 1971. In *Congressional Behavior*, ed. Nelson W. Polsby. New York: Random House.

"The Electoral Arena." 1973. In *The Congress and America's Future*, 2d ed., ed. David B. Truman. Englewood Cliffs, N.J.: Prentice-Hall.

"Micro and Macro Politics." 1968. In *Political Theory and Political Research: Essays for V. O. Key*, ed. Oliver Garceau. Cambridge: Harvard University Press.

"Rise and Decline of One-Party Systems in United States." 1970. In *Authoritarian Politics in Modern Society*, ed. Samuel P. Huntington. New York: Basic Books.

"Computer Simulation and Legislative 'Professionalism'." 1975. In *Congress in Change*, ed. Norman J. Ornstein. New York: Praeger. Originally prepared for the 1970 APSA meetings; somewhat abbreviated version appears as Chapter 1 in the Ornstein book.

"'Critical Elections' and Party History: A Critical View." 1971. *Polity* (Winter): 236-42.

"Voter Response to Short-Run Economic Conditions: Asymmetric Effect of Prosperity and Recession." 1975. *American Political Science Review* 69 (December): 1240-54. (with Howard Bloom).

"Careers and Committees in the American Congress: The Problem of Structural Change." 1977. In *History of Parliamentary Behavior*, ed.

William Aydelotte. Princeton, N.J.: Princeton University Press-Math Social Sciences Board, 28-62.

"Who Opposed Woman Suffrage? An Analysis of State Referenda Voting. 1910-1918." Paper for 1982 APSA meeting (with Eileen McDonagh).

"Woman Suffrage in the Progressive Era: Patterns of Opposition and Support in Referenda Voting, 1910-1918." 1985. *American Political Science Review* 79:415-35 (with Eileen McDonagh).

Newly Published in this Volume

"History of Ethics in Congress: Three Perspectives."
"House Turnover and the Counterrevolution to Rotation in Office."
"New Perspectives on Wilson's Congressional Government."
"Organizing by Party, Committees by Seniority, and Voting by Coalition."

INDEX

Abram, Michael, 69
Adams, Henry, 146
Adams, John, 106
Adams, Samuel, 92
Alaska, 116
Aldrich, Nelson, 49
Alexander, DeAlva S., 70
Alley, John B., 137
Allison, William Boyd, 137
Ames, Oakes, 136-38
Aristotle, 80
Arkansas, 116
Army Engineers (1949), 185,
  (1952), 186
Arthur, Chester A., 147
Atomic Energy Act (1954), 186

Bagehot, Walter, 14-16, 149, 155
Bailey, Joseph W., 39
Baker, E. D., 89, 90
Bankhead, William B., 35
Banking and Currency Committee,
  41
Barkley, Alben, 35, 51
Bayard, James A., 137
Bentley, Arthur F., 170-71
Benton, Thomas Hart, 39
Beyle, Herman, 162, 180-81
Biddle, Nicholas, 67
Bidwell, Barnabas, 150
Bilbo, Theodore, 50
Bingham, John A., 137
Blaine, James G., 38, 42, 137, 153
Bolling, Richard, 131
Borah, William, 50
Bricker, John, 171
Brooks, James, 138
Brownell, Herbert, 39
Bruns, Roger, 130, 136

Bryan, William Jennings, 19, 30,
  34, 110
Bryce, James, 91, 155
Buchanan, William, 115
Burke, Edmund, 55
Burr, Aaron, 132
Byrns, Joseph W., 35

Calhoun, John C., 59, 132
Campbell, Angus, 14
Cannon, Clarence, 41
Cannon, Joseph, 30, 43-44, 46, 67,
  69, 70, 111-13, 116, 121, 125,
  153
Capehart, Homer, 173
Carlisle, John G., 38, 42, 153-54
Carroll, Charles, 57-58
Celler, Emanuel, 30
Chicago, 24
Chrysler Building, 168-69
Citizens' Research Foundation, 25
Clapp, Charles L., 21
Clark, Joseph, 16, 49, 57
Clay, Henry, 38, 43, 57, 59, 110
Cleveland, Grover, 41, 156
Colfax, Schuyler, 137, 153
Columbus, Christopher, 149
Compromise of 1850, 43
Confirmation of "Liberal"
  Appointees (1949), 185
Congressional Quarterly, 130
Control of Subversion (1954), 186
Cooper, Fenimore, 92
Cooper, Joseph, 69
Cordon, Guy, 173
Cox, S. S. ("Sunset"), 68
Credit Mobiliér, 136, 138, 139
Credit Mobiliér Scandal (1873),
  136

Crisp, Charles F., 38, 40, 42, 68, 108
Crittenden, John J., 58
Curvin, Henry F., 118
Dallinger, Frederick W., 91
Darwin, Charles, 71
Dawes, Henry L., 42, 137
Derge, David, 121
Dies, Martin, 135
Dingley, Nelson, 68
Dionisopoulos, P. A., 129
Dirksen, Everett M., 39
Douglas, Stephen A., 39, 50, 59, 64
Drew, Elizabeth, 139

Eastland, James O., 5
Economic Controls (Defense Production Act) (1950), 185, (1953), 186
Eisenhower, Dwight D., 39, 42, 139, 187
Elazar, Daniel, 134
Elections and Party Management (Hanham), 130
Ellender, Allen, 191
Empire State Building, 169
Engle, Clair, 39
Erikson, Kai, 131
Eulau, Heinz, 72, 121
Extend Rent Control (1952), 186

Federal Election Campaign Practices Act (1972), 26
Federal Road Aid (1952), 186
FEPC legislation, 189
Fiorina, Morris, 63
Fish, C. R., 94
Ford, Henry Jones, 155-57, 166
Fulbright, J. William, 179

Gallatin, Albert, 57

"Galton's Problem," 114
Garceau, Oliver, 55
Garfield, James A., 42, 110, 137, 147
Garner, John N., 35
Gillet, Frederick, H., 38
Glenn, John, 50
Goldwater, Barry, 182
Goldwater Disaster, 117
Gore, Albert, Sr., 191
Gorman, Arthur, 49
Grant, Ulysses S., 147
Greeley, Horace, 91
Green, John Richard, 148
Greenstein, Fred, 139-40
Grimes, James W., 137
Guggenheim Museum, 168-69
Guttman, Louis, 162, 167-69, 173

Hamilton, Alexander, 106
Hamilton, James, Jr., 131-32
Hammond, Jabez, 96
Hanham, H. J., 130
Hardin, John J., 89
Harding, Warren G., 71
Harrington, James, 80, 100
Hay, John, 89-90
Hayden, Carl, 39
Hayes, Rutherford B., 147
Haynes, George, 118, 122
Hell's Canyon, 163
Hiscock, Frank, 42
Hoar, George Frisbie, 150
Holcombe, Arthur, 155
Holman, William, 42, 109, 110
Hooper, Samuel, 137
Houghton Mifflin, 143
Houston, Sam, 133-34, 140
Hudson River, 132
Hyneman, Charles, 72, 120, 121

Jackson, Andrew, 66-67, 72, 88, 100, 115, 133-34, 155
Jacksonian development of the presidency, 156
Javits, Jacob, 51
Jefferson, Thomas, 66, 72, 76, 106, 115, 150
Jenckes, Thomas Allen, 93
Johns Hopkins University, 143
Johnson, Andrew, 147
Johnson, Lyndon, 42, 51,
Jones, Charles O., 16
Jourdain, M. (Molière), 164

Keating, Kenneth, 39, 51
Kefauver, Estes, 31, 191
Keifer, John, 42
Kelley, William D. ("Pig-Iron"), 138
Kennedy family, 50
Kennedy, John F., 42, 51, 131
Kennedy, Robert, 7, 50
Kentucky, 116
Kern, John W., 65-66
Kernell, Samuel, 78-79, 88, 95, 96-99
Kerr, Clara H., 64
Kerr, Michael, 42-43, 51, 68
Key, V. O., 14, 17
Kiernan, James H., 118
Kirwan, Michael J., 29
Kramer, Gerald, 8-9

LaFollette, Bob, Jr., 31, 50-51, 71, 124
LaFollette-Monroney Act (1946), 39
LaGuardia, Fiorello, 71
Lee, Richard Henry, 71, 81, 92
Lincoln, Abraham, 50, 89-90, 92
Lockard, Duane, 117

Logan, John A., 137
Logan, Steven, 90
Long family, 50
Long, Russell, 27, 191
Louis XVI, 99
Lowell, A. Lawrence, 156

Madison, James, 57
Magnuson, Warren, 171
Mahon, George, 41
Malone, George, 182
Mann, James, 67
Marcy, William, 97
Markov model, 53
Martin, Thomas S., 65-66
Mason, George, 77, 81
Matthews, Donald R., 23
McCarthy, Joseph, 31, 139, 140
McCarthyism, 139
McClellan, John, 171
McConachie, Lauros, 64, 109, 121
McCormack, John, 35, 41
McKinley, William, 42
McMillin, Benton, 40, 108
McNary, Charles, 51
Michener, James A., 24
Michigan, 24
Mills, Roger, 40, 108-09
Mills, Wilbur, 41
Morgan, John T., 49
Morningstar, Richard, 59, 60
Morrill, Justin, 39
Morrison, William H., 42, 68
Morton, Thruston, 51
Murphy, George, 50

Namier, Lewis, 130
National Bank, 67
Nebraska, 114
Neustadt, Richard, 135
New Deal, 12, 27, 30

New Jersey, 115
New Mexico, 116
New Politics, 30
Nicolay, John G., 89-90
Nixon, Richard M., 39, 51
Norris, George, 50, 111-12
North Carolina, 115
Nye, Gerald P., 31

O'Connor, John, 35
Ohio, 24
Ombudsman, 27
Ostrogorski, M., 156
Ottinger, Richard, 25

Patterson, James, 138
Patterson, Tom, 49
Pawtucket, 118
Payne, Sereno, 69
Pepper, Claude, 191
Philadelphia, 24
Polk, James K., 133
Polsby, Nelson W., 61, 68-69, 95, 139
Postal Pay Increase (1955), 186
Powell, Adam Clayton, 129
Pred, Alan R., 133
Profiles in Courage (Kennedy), 131
Progressives, 111-12, 124

Quine, Willard V. O., 167

Rainey, Henry T., 35
Randall, Samuel, 68, 109, 153
Randolph, Edmund, 80
Rangel, Charles, 6
Rayburn, Sam, 33, 51, 104
Reagan, Ronald, 144
Reciprocal Trade Act Extension (1949), 185

Reed, Thomas Brackett, 42-43, 46, 69, 112, 153
Regulars, 111
Rent Control Act, 181
Revenue Act (1950), 189
Revenue Code (1954), 186
Rice, Stuart, 61, 162, 180
Riker, William, 49
Rockefeller, Nelson, 25
Rocky Mountain West, 5
Rohde, David, 63
Roll Call, 122
Roosevelt, Franklin D., 22, 41-42, 124, 156; New Deal, 12, 27, 30
Rossiter, Clinton, 135
Rubber Plant Disposal (1953), 186
Rules Committee, 112, 117
Russell, Carl, 92
Russell, Richard, 51

Salinger, Pierre, 7, 33, 49
Sayers, Joseph, 43
Schattschneider, E. E., 19, 61, 86
Schlesinger, Arthur, Jr., 130, 136
Scolfield, Glenn W., 137
Seventeenth Amendment, 50
Sherman, John, 39
Silverman, Corrine, 55
Smathers, George, 51
Smith, Al, 61
Smith, Howard, 104, 166
Sorauf, Frank, 21
Spanish-American War, 42
Spooner, John C., 48
Springer, William, 34, 40, 68, 108, 109, 110
Stanberry, William, 133-34, 140
Stevens, Thaddeus, 67, 147
Stokes, Donald E., 8, 12

The Structure of Politics at the Accession of George III (Namier), 130
Sumner, Charles, 39, 64
Sumner, William Graham, 140
Survey Research Center, 14

Taft family, 50
Taft Hartley Act, 182
Taft, William Howard, 112
Talmadge, 50
Teapot Dome Scandal, 31
Thatcher, Margaret, 144
Thermidorean Reaction, 99
Tillman, Ben, ("Pitchfork"), 64-66
Turner, Julius, 164
Truman, Harry S., 42, 51, 135, 182

Underwood, Oscar W., 39
Union Pacific, 138
Universal Military Training (1951), 185

Van Buren, Martin, 96
Vardeman, James K., 50
Vinson, Carl, 34, 42
Viola, Herman J., 133

Wagner, Robert, 31
Wahlke, John, 72, 121
Walsh, Tom, 31
Washington, D.C., 147
Washington, George, 106, 115
Watson, Tom, 50, 51
Ways and Means Committee, 112
Weldon, Joseph, 33
Wellman, Walter, 48
Whitridge, Frederic, 94
Wilkinson, Bud, 50
Williams, John Sharp, 39
Wilson, Henry, 137

Wilson, James F., 137
Wilson, William, 38, 41
Wilson, Woodrow, 22, 64, 65, 67, 112, 124, 143-57
Wissel, Peter, 63
Witmer, Richard T., 95
Witt, Stuart, 116
Wood, Fernando, 42, 68
Wright, Silas, 97
Wyatt-Brown, Bertram, 132

Young, James, 81, 91, 110

Zeller, Belle, 72, 114, 119